G000123358

Frank Ryan

HISTORICAL ASSOCIATION OF IRELAND

LIFE AND TIMES

NEW SERIES

General Editor: Ciaran Brady

Now available
Frank Ryan by Fearghal McGarry
Michael Davitt by Carla King
Thomas Kettle by Senia Pašeta
John Mitchel by James Quinn
Denis Guiney by Peter Costello

Titles are in preparation on Sir Edward Carson,
Joseph McGrath and James Clarence Mangan.

Frank Ryan

FEARGHAL McGARRY

✳

Published on behalf of
the Historical Association of Ireland
by

UNIVERSITY COLLEGE DUBLIN PRESS
Preas Choláiste Ollscoile Bhaile Átha Cliath
2010

First published 2002 on behalf of the
Historical Association of Ireland by Dundalgan Press, Dundalk
This revised edition published 2010 by
University College Dublin Press

ISBN 978-1-906359-36-2
ISSN 2009-1397

University College Dublin Press
Newman House, 86 St Stephen's Green
Dublin 2, Ireland
www.ucdpress.ie

Cataloguing in Publication data available from the British Library

Typeset in Northumberland in Ehrhardt by Seton-Burberry
Text design by Lyn Davies
Printed in England on acid-free paper by
CPI Antony Rowe, Chippenham

CONTENTS

FOREWORD

Originally conceived over a decade ago to place the lives of leading figures in Irish history against the background of new research on the problems and conditions of their times and modern assessments of their historical significance, the Historical Association of Ireland Life and Times series enjoyed remarkable popularity and success. A second series has now been planned in association with UCD Press in a new format and with fuller scholarly apparatus. Encouraged by the reception given to the earlier series, the volumes in the new series will be expressly designed to be of particular help to students preparing for the Leaving Certificate, for GCE Advanced Level and for undergraduate history courses as well as appealing to the happily insatiable appetite for new views of Irish history among the general public.

CIARAN BRADY
Historical Association of Ireland

PREFACE

I am grateful to Ciaran Brady and Colm Croker for producing the original edition of this book, and Barbara Mennell and Noelle Moran of UCD Press for their work on this revised edition. R. V. Comerford kindly commented on the original manuscript. Conversations with Frank Ryan's friends – Elizabeth Clissmann, Eugene Downing and Nora Harkin – were of great help. Mark Hull, Brian Hanley, David O'Donoghue, Barry McLoughlin, Eunan O'Halpin and Margaret Ó hÓgartaigh generously shared their research. It benefited also from responses to papers read at St Patrick's College, Drumcondra, Hertford College, Oxford, and the Irish Historical Society. Thanks also to Tim Pat Coogan, James Hopkins, Paul Preston, Richard Baxell, Éanna Ó Caollaí, Wendy Davies, David Baxter, David Timmons and Selina Walsh. I would like to acknowledge the support of the Department of Modern History, NUI Maynooth, and the Irish Research Council for the Humanities and Social Sciences.

Cover image of Frank Ryan in Republican Spain, October 1937, is reproduced courtesy of the Fifteenth International Brigade Photographic Unit Photographs Collection, Abraham Lincoln Brigade Archives, Tamiment Library, New York University.

FEARGHAL McGARRY
School of History and Anthropology
Queen's University Belfast
May 2010

CHRONOLOGY OF RYAN'S LIFE AND TIMES

1902

11 September: Frank Ryan born at Elton, near Knocklong, County Limerick.

1916

Easter Rising occurs.

1919

War of Independence begins; Ryan may have taken part.

1921

Enters UCD; War of Independence ended by truce and Anglo-Irish Treaty.

1922

Ryan joins anti-Treatyites in Irish Civil War; interned by Provisional Government forces.

1923

Civil War ends; Ryan released from Curragh and resumes studies.

1925

Graduates from UCD and intensifies republican activism.

1926

Appointed adjutant of Dublin Brigade, IRA; organises demonstration against O'Casey's *The Plough and the Stars*.

1929

Elected member of IRA executive; succeeds Peadar O'Donnell as editor of *An Phoblacht*.

1931

IRA forms left-wing party, Saor Éire, leading to coercion of IRA by Cumann na nGaedheal Government; Ryan imprisoned in Arbour Hill.

1932
Fianna Fáil elected to government; IRA coercion suspended.

1933
Rise of the Blueshirts; communist headquarters attacked; Jim Gralton deported; increasing tensions between IRA's left-wing, including Ryan, and leadership; Ryan resigns from *An Phoblacht* and IRA executive.

1934
Left-wing republicans, including Ryan, leave IRA to establish unsuccessful Republican Congress.

1936
Spanish Civil War begins; Ryan leads contingent of Irishmen to fight in the International Brigades.

1938
Ryan captured by Italian forces and imprisoned in Burgos; Ryan's death sentence commuted to life imprisonment.

1939
Nazi-Soviet Non-Aggression Pact; Second World War begins.

1940
General Franco releases Ryan to German military intelligence; Ryan and IRA chief of staff, Seán Russell, brought to Irish coast by U-boat but return without landing after death of Russell.

1940–4
Ryan remains in Germany as an adviser on Irish affairs.

1944
10 June: Ryan dies in a sanatorium in Loschwitz near Dresden after long period of declining health.

1979
Ryan's remains reinterred in Glasnevin Cemetery, Dublin.

ABBREVIATIONS

ACA	Army Comrades Association
CID	Criminal Investigation Department (Dublin Metropolitan Police)
CP	Communist Party
CPI	Communist Party of Ireland
DDR	German Democratic Republic
ETA	Euskadi Ta Askatasuna
FS	Free State
GHQ	General Headquarters
ICA	Irish Citizen Army
INLA	Irish National Liberation Army
IRA	Irish Republican Army
MP	Member of Parliament
MS	Manuscript
NLI	National Library of Ireland
POUM	Partido Obrero Unificación Marxista
PRO	UK Public Record Office (now The National Archives)
RJD	Rosamond Jacob diary
SS	Schutzstaffel (Nazi Party militia)
TU	Trade Union
UCD	University College Dublin
UCDA	University College Dublin Archives

CHAPTER I

Republican, 1902–32

Frank Ryan was born at Elton, near Knocklong, County Limerick, on 11 September 1902. His parents, Vere Ryan and Anne Slattery, were schoolteachers. Both were from modest backgrounds – Vere was the son of a Limerick teacher, and Anne the daughter of a small farmer from Clare; but their nine children – or at least the boys – benefited from the greater opportunities of the times. Two of Ryan's brothers – Vincent and Maurice – qualified as doctors; Jeremiah became a teacher; while John, whom Frank described as the 'black sheep' of the family, worked as a labourer in the United States. Three of Ryan's sisters, Mary, Catherine and Anne, became nuns while the youngest, Eilís, a graduate, worked in the registry of University College Dublin.

Ryan demonstrated the spirited side to his personality early in life. His sister Eilís recalled 'how he used to break everything and get blamed for it – and how he ran away from school twice'.[1] Ryan remembered 'escaping through the window from his father's school', and later boarding at St Colman's College in Fermoy, being at the receiving end of floggings for smoking and truancy.[2] But Ryan also displayed a more thoughtful side to his character. He developed a deep enthusiasm for the Irish language of the Gaeltacht. Later, perhaps an early indication of his idealism, he felt he had a vocation and began attending the Holy Ghost Fathers' Rockwell College. But his rebellious streak led to his expulsion for protesting against the food in the college, and he returned to St Colman's to complete his secondary education.

Ryan did not inherit his radicalism: his devout mother was apolitical, while his father had been a politically inactive Parnellite. Nor was East Limerick, dominated by big farmers, particularly republican. Yet even at school Ryan considered himself a 'hot republican', attributing this, like his love of Irish, to the influence of his older brother, Vincent, and one of the priests at St Colman's. Eilís recollected:

> There was a priest there called Father Roche who was a mad republi-
> can. Frank was very easily influenced and he did what he was told.
> Jumped back out over the wall at night to drill. Maurice [Frank's
> brother] who was with him . . . wouldn't be led by anyone. That's
> where Frank got it . . . Frank was impressionable; he'd believe anything.
> Maurice was sensible.[3]

But Ryan's republicanism was not unusual, considering he came of age during the Irish revolution. He was 13 at the time of the Easter Rising of 1916, and 17 when Sinn Féin swept aside the Irish Parliamentary Party in the 1918 General Election. Little is known about his early involvement in the republican movement. His friends believed he played little or no role in the War of Independence, but Ryan claimed that he joined the East Limerick Brigade of the IRA at 16 – around the beginning of the War of Independence – and was appointed an officer at 18.[4] His sister, Eilís, believed he joined the IRA when he left school after the 1921 Truce. Given the poor image of the 'trucileers' and his later prominence in a leadership dominated by 1916 and War of Independence veterans, Ryan may have exaggerated what was probably a peripheral involvement in the war.

In the autumn of 1921, as Sinn Féin negotiated with the British government and the disagreements within its leadership became more apparent, Ryan began studying for a degree in Celtic Studies in University College Dublin. When the Civil War began the following summer, Eilís saw her brother cycling off with two men towards the gunfire in Kilmallock. In September Ryan was wounded, captured and sent to Limerick Jail. He was interned in the Curragh, where he discovered a talent for journalism through editing the Irish-language camp magazine; for much of his life Ryan worked as a journalist, editor and printer of radical newspapers. However, his internment aggravated a painful childhood ear illness which rendered him partially deaf, a condition which continued to deteriorate throughout his life.[5] After his release in November 1923, and the restoration of his county council scholarship, Ryan returned to UCD, where he edited the Gaelic Society's journal and co-founded the university's Republican Club. He graduated in 1925 and began studying for a master's degree, but soon drifted into full-time republican activism.

The mid-1920s was a demoralising period for republicans. Morale was shattered by defeat in the Civil War. Many of the republican leadership had been killed, while the 15,000 republican internees released in 1924 were faced with unemployment and discrimination by the pro-Treaty government. Public support for Sinn Féin proved initially resilient but subsequently declined, prompting de Valera's formation of Fianna Fáil in 1926. As before, the IRA and Sinn Féin had overlapping memberships. Both were united in opposition to the Treaty and the Irish Free State, but there were important differences. Most significantly, the IRA saw its role as a military one and lacked much interest, or faith, in political means. Most IRA men continued to support Sinn Féin (and later Fianna Fáil), but there was considerable resentment against the 'politicians', who were blamed for the disastrous turn of events since 1921. This militarist outlook was strengthened by the IRA's reorganisation in 1925, when it withdrew allegiance from the emergency republican

government which had been theoretically established during the
Civil War and vested authority in its own Army Council. The IRA
was reorganised as a secret army whose principal opponent was the
Irish Free State rather than Britain. Its activities consisted of little
more than recruiting, training and sporadic violence. Although cap-
able of shocking acts, such as the assassination of Kevin O'Higgins,
it remained too weak to threaten the Free State.

One effect of the Civil War defeat, reinforced by Cumann na
nGaedheal's coercion, was to bind the remaining rump of active
republicans into a close-knit community. Ryan's work, activism
and socialising – with the distinctions between them blurred – took
place within republican circles. He worked for republican-owned
businesses, wrote for republican newspapers, organised Irish lec-
tures and *céilithe* and worked his way up the IRA. In October 1925
Ryan began teaching night classes for the Gaelic League and met
the writer Rosamond Jacob, an agnostic Quaker, and (like her close
friend Hanna Sheehy Skeffington) a middle-class intellectual, femi-
nist, republican and pacifist. Her causes included anti-imperialism,
animal rights, anticlericalism and support for the Soviet Union.
(This did not always lead to an entirely consistent outlook – Jacob
rejoiced at the assassination of Kevin O'Higgins in 1927 but felt
that the anti-imperialist meetings attracted 'nasty smoking spit-
ting type of men'.)[6]

Jacob soon fell in love with Ryan – 'you could learn anything from
him, his mixture of intense interest and knowledge and natural
equal simplicity is so delicious, combined with the pleasure of looking at him.'[7] Despite some differences (Ryan was 23 when he met the
more sophisticated 37-year-old Jacob), he was also attracted to her.
They began a sexual relationship which, for Jacob at least, brought
pain as well as happiness. Ryan insisted on secrecy, even to the extent
of sometimes ignoring Jacob at social events. Their nights together
were infrequent; in some years, much to her despair, as rarely as two

or three occasions. The practical difficulties posed by Jacob's vigilant landlady were surmounted by stealth – 'The black panther [Ryan] came in noiselessly a little before 12 and was more delicious than ever' – or secret meetings – 'Made love eagerly for nearly an hour . . . but it was a horrid uncomfortable place . . . a motor car is infernally cramped.'[8] But Ryan's sense of guilt and lack of intimacy were greater problems. In 1929 Jacob noted: 'He was lovely – but how insanely ambivalent he is – This must stop! – Do you think I'd come here if I didn't like it? . . . He was so miserable, so sick with himself, so ashamed & downhearted . . . if only he'd be reasonable & articulate – but it's so cruel not to be able to give him any comfort beyond the moment, to have him blame himself for giving way to his desires instead of letting me be permanent friends.'[9] Jacob approved of 'free love' but Ryan appeared more constrained by his Catholic morality. The following month Jacob wrote: 'As to black panther, I had hell from him, in suspense, disappointment and starvation, but I had a few heavenly hours to make up, – but if only his soul was more friendly – I sometimes feel that as he wants me physically he doesn't want me to talk to – the shyness & the sense of sin he seems to get, & I helpless to prevent it.'[10] Part of the attraction for Ryan may have been for a physical relationship without emotional ties. Even in private, Jacob noted, he was often withdrawn: 'He was inaccessible as usual . . . but finally asked me not to talk'; 'I think it's too bad never to come except for that. It's not fair.'[11] In 1930 she wrote: 'I haven't yet succeeded in getting through the wall of reserve that encompasses him. He has given me a good deal of confidence and a little love, but so little of his company . . . I love him rather more than ever.' She never did succeed. Their sexual relationship ended in the mid-1930s, but they remained life-long friends, and Jacob strove to protect Ryan's legacy after his death when others did not.

Ryan's allure was partly due to his gunman image. Jacob was enthralled by his stories of 'wild incidents of the war' and a dramatic occasion when he asked her to hide some documents: 'the thought of P[roinnsias] as an armed desperado is very intriguing.'[12] But although Ryan had little difficulty in attracting women, he was less successful with relationships. He fell in love with Kevin Barry's sister Elgin, but she married The O'Rahilly. His fiancée, Bobbie Walshe, left him, later marrying Frank Edwards. Ryan was not only attractive to women on a romantic level. He was more egalitarian than his contemporaries in masculine IRA circles and inclined to accept women as political and intellectual equals. His charismatic personality was also an important aspect of his appeal to men. He was hero-worshipped by younger republicans and admired by most who knew him. But he was also resented for a perceived arrogance: Geoffrey Coulter, assistant editor of *An Phoblacht*, described him as a man with the swagger 'of the absolutely fearless young male – a trait that excites too much envy'.[13] But for most people, Ryan was a likeable figure and genuinely popular even among his opponents. A close friend, Elizabeth 'Budge' Clissmann, recalled driving through Dublin in Ryan's distinctive Sunbeam open-top car and being amazed by how many of the gardaí on traffic duty greeted Ryan with a grin and salute.[14] Jacob noted Ryan's attitude to the most hated figure in Special Branch, Superintendent Peter Ennis, with similar surprise after a court acquittal: 'P. came out, & chatted happily & pleasantly with them nearly 5 minutes. Certainly one can't hope to understand men.'[15] The youthful Ryan was a likeable, if rather wild figure ('a lunatic', Jacob admiringly wrote), passionately devoted to republicanism but also very much a social animal. His life involved police persecution, endless meetings and unpaid work, but was convivial enough in other respects, allowing freedom from the boredom of conventional work, much socialising, drinking, dancing and a degree of notoriety.

After graduating, Ryan attempted to establish a teaching career, but, despite his enthusiasm for Irish, his deafness proved too great

a handicap. Despite numerous operations, his hearing deteriorated
to the point where he had to rely on lip-reading or people to shout
in his ear. He gave up teaching after being rejected for a position at
the new teacher-training colleges: he had been unable to hear the
interviewer's questions. Ryan felt guilty about his failure to hold
down a job: 'He said he wasn't going to try teaching jobs any more –
its only making a fool of himself – & his father will be annoyed &
disappointed, he keeps expecting so much of him.' To his annoy-
ance, a younger sister, who wanted to study music, had to follow
her two sisters into the convent. Jacob noted: 'It doesn't seem
much pleasure to him to go home – it's "a worry" – they keep
wondering why he doesn't have a good job and get on; he having
been the most brilliant one of the family.'[16] Ryan turned to
journalism, editing a travel magazine and – by night – the IRA's *An
t-Óglach*. His main ambition, however, was to found an Irish-
language newspaper.

The mid-1920s were an important period in the development of
Irish republicanism. The Civil War had thrown together disparate
factions under the banner of anti-Treaty Sinn Féin; within the
party could be found extremists such as Mary MacSwiney who
rejected any compromise short of a sovereign republic, alongside
more moderate politicians like de Valera. By the mid-1920s tensions between these groups were surfacing on the issue of Sinn
Féin's attitude to the Irish Free State. De Valera argued that republicans must come to terms with the state's existence and attempt to
win public support for their views even if that meant entering the
Free State Dáil, which republicans regarded as illegitimate. The
MacSwiney faction continued to consider only those deputies who
had remained true to the Republic – that is, themselves – as the
legitimate government. This had the virtue of consistency, but
ignored the fact that the Irish electorate increasingly accepted the
legitimacy of the new state. In March 1926 de Valera's faction split

from Sinn Féin to form Fianna Fáil. As in the Civil War, social factors were not particularly significant. The post-de Valera Sinn Féin espoused an extreme nationalism, but was Catholic and conservative in its social outlook. Fianna Fáil was more socially radical, but combined conservatives like de Valera alongside more modernising politicians like Seán Lemass. The IRA stood somewhat detached from both. Its volunteers could be found supporting both, but most IRA men regarded political methods as inferior to physical-force republicanism. As with the two political parties, social issues were secondary – IRA membership spanned from right-wing bigots to communists.

Where did Ryan stand during this period of schism? Jacob met him outside the Rotunda on the night of the stormy *ard-fheis* in March 1926 when Sinn Féin split: 'He disapproves of the proposals, but knows we couldn't get on without DeV . . . He said something very disreputable about wanting to go out with a gun again.'[17] He expressed similar sentiments months later: 'He doesn't believe in [Fianna Fáil] . . . if they did get a majority the F[ree] S[tate] & all its institutions w[oul]d still be there – nothing for it but the gun.'[18] Ryan believed the unfinished revolution was a military rather than a political problem. As he declared in a funeral oration at Milltown cemetery, 'Ireland, held in subjection by force, can be freed only by meeting that force with greater force and thus defeating it. To-day, as in every other generation, the soldiers must be henceforward our primary concern, for they alone can bring freedom and peace.'[19] As later *An Phoblacht* editorials demonstrated, he saw physical force as not only necessary but morally superior to other forms of struggle:

> Thus it was after the failure of the Fenian revolt of 1867: one leader seeking a new alignment, pinned his faith to an agrarian movement; another pinned his to parliamentary agitation. Neither faith was the

true national faith, so neither faith – even when embraced by millions – led the nation to freedom.[20]

Ryan's use of the word 'faith' was apposite. His belief in physical force was rooted in a near-religious devotion to the creed which Pearse's writings and subsequent martyrdom had made central to militant republicanism. Ryan's pamphlet on the Easter Rising, published in 1928, demonstrated the extent of his Pearsean worldview. Ten years on, the First World War was still viewed approvingly: 'Patriotism and patriotism alone moved the rival peoples . . . Nationality reared its head proudly in the welter of war, and the men of each country gladly fought and died for it.' Quiescent Ireland, in contrast, 'lay in shame' until, in 1916, 'great-souled men had, Christ-like, to lay down their lives'. For Ryan, the lesson of 1916 was utterly simple:

> The road we tread leads to war – war for Ireland against her only enemy, the British Empire. To that end, we concentrate all our energies in arming, equipping and training. We who have lived in 1916, who have triumphed in 1921, who have known defeat in 1923, we shall not go to our graves until that defeat be redeemed, until the shame that Ireland suffers be wiped out, when we again raise the flag in battle in our generation.[21]

Even by the standards of the time, Ryan's unbridled admiration for physical force was extreme and, at times, mindlessly simplistic; at one public meeting 'He asked his audience to judge every cause by the one good criterion, "Were the supporters of that cause willing to fight for it?" If they are willing, that cause is good'.[22]

Aside from physical force, the importance of the Irish language and culture formed a key aspect of Ryan's outlook. Organising *céilithe* and teaching Irish formed part of his political activism, but, in contrast to his political views, Ryan did not sympathise with the language extremists within the Irish-Ireland movement. Although the Gaelic League had flourished in the late nineteenth century, the popularity of the once vibrant voluntary movement declined after the establishment of the Irish Free State. The state's policy of enforced gaelicisation in the school and workplace failed, and a more strident tendency towards exclusiveness and insularity became evident within the Irish-Ireland movement. This was not shared by Ryan, who emphasised the need for 'gaiety & lightness in the branch' at Gaelic League meetings. He organised jazz dances for his Republican Club, an activity frowned upon by Irish-Ireland extremists; one of his more dour Gaeilgeoir acquaintances, the butt of Ryan's jibes for kilt-wearing, even considered him a 'seoinín'. Ryan was even less keen on native speakers, whom he found 'more slippery' than parvenus like himself.[23]

In 1927 Ryan attempted to combine militarism and gaelicism in his unsuccessful organisation An Pobal. Jacob's diary gives a flavour of the meetings:

> He began by asserting we had peace now & couldn't have freedom till we destroyed that peace . . . and he went on about the Gaelic League & the way it betrayed itself when it ceased to be political . . . He was very clear about the sort of Republic wanted. It was all interesting & all characteristic, & slightly fanatical, his insistence on everything being a waste of time that isn't preparing for a fight.[24]

Some months later, during the general election campaign of September 1927 which saw Fianna Fáil enter the Dáil and hence the tacit recognition of the Free State by the largest section of anti-Treaty republicanism, Ryan wrote to Jacob:

Tell me, have you too got election fever? For me, I was never so disgusted with talk. I read the rival advertisements in the paper, that's all. Of course, I want to see Cosgrave beaten, but the price we're paying for that is degrading. Fianna Fáil's policy is futile. It can never give us more than a better Free State . . . I've only one use for our 153 deputies: if I could I'd gather them all up and swap them for 153 pieces of artillery – or even 3, if I got them.

Ryan combined an unsophisticated extremism – and a contempt for politics common within the IRA – with a relatively astute analysis of the limitations of Fianna Fáil's programme:

The Oath will go, and the Safety Bill with it. But that's all. (I'm dogmatic but I bet you I'm right). Honestly, I can't take sides in what I consider a domestic row between moderates. I'm more concerned with trying to hold together the remnants of the 100 per cent revolutionaries, so that there will be someone left to talk – at least – of Lalor and Connolly . . . What maddens me is that (if and) when Éamon de Valera rules the Free State that programme will be all the harder to realise. But enough politics, I feel so mad about them that I want to wear a red shirt and bomb politicians of all degrees. I'm twenty-five years today. Before I'm twenty-six I hope to have straightened out much of this crooked life of mine, and to have got beyond the talking-stage in many things.[25]

Ryan's outlook was extreme by Irish standards, but was less so in the context of European politics. The IRA's enthusiasm for violence, extreme nationalism and disgust for constitutional politics were not exceptional in the radical political discourse of inter-war Europe – particularly among groups supported by veterans of the First World War or its revolutionary aftermath. As Mark Mazower noted, the rise of nationalism, communism and fascism radically weakened public belief in liberal democracy in the 1920s: 'Anti-liberal and anti-democratic creeds had been gaining ground since the last quarter of the nineteenth century. In the wake of the Great War, they spread fast, through a "gospel of violence" most visible in the Fascist movement but common to many members of what a later historian was to call the "generation of 1914". Reared on war, extremist ideologues preferred violence to reason, action to rhetoric . . . Many young European males in the 1920s seemed ready to justify and even advocate the politics of confrontation.'[26] The experience of IRA men, who had lived through war, revolution and civil war had much in common with the revolutionary ferment which produced the extremist politics of inter-war Europe, although other factors which fuelled radical continental movements were absent in Britain and Ireland.

Ryan's reference to Lalor and Connolly indicate the importance of social radicalism to him. Fintan Lalor's central theme, frequently endorsed by Ryan, was the necessity for the 'reconquest of Ireland'. As England had oppressed Ireland not only politically but economically, genuine freedom meant not only a national but also a social revolution. James Connolly's achievement, as Ryan saw it, was to combine socialism with physical-force nationalism – he liked to call 'for less talk about Connolly and for more of Connolly's methods'.[27] But despite this, it would be inaccurate to view Ryan as a socialist in the same way as contemporaries such as Peadar O'Donnell. Tom Barry was more accurate in his description of Ryan as 'a patriotic Irish Republican' whose left-wing sympathies were based on the Irish radical tradition.[28] One important distinction between Ryan and O'Donnell was the latter's scepticism towards physical force. Whereas O'Donnell's career was dedicated to weaning republicanism from this preoccupation, Ryan wished to combine social radicalism with militarism. Ryan was genuinely influenced by nineteenth-century patriots such as

Mitchel and Lalor, but O'Donnell, more communistic in outlook, tended to crudely raid this tradition to apply a green gloss to his red politics. O'Donnell only expressed communist ideas in republican terminology because most republicans viewed explicit class politics with suspicion. For example, he substituted the concept of the 'Gael' (the pre-Plantation western peasant) for Marx's incorruptible working class – leading to slightly absurd editorials calling for 'The Dictatorship of the Gael'.[29] The problem with this, as Richard English has pointed out, was that it led to an incoherent and sectarian merger of republicanism and Marxism which excluded the Protestant working class.[30] For example, in 1929 when a new IRA party called for 'the clean, Gaelic, Christian mind of Ireland [to] . . . revolt against the beastliness of English Imperial paganism', *An Phoblacht* noted:

> Gaelicism, as Pádraig MacPiarais taught us, is not merely a matter of externals. An English spy may learn and speak the Irish tongue as an aid to his profession – he does not thereby become a Gael. Gaelicism, if it is to have any meaning in the world of facts, must be the rejection by the Irish people of the whole English civilisation – and the building of our future upon the roots of our past – upon those roots that gripped our soil before the 'Conquest'.[31]

Although the leaders of the IRA's emerging left, such as the northern Presbyterian George Gilmore, were genuinely non-sectarian, it is difficult to see how this implicitly ethnic formulation could appeal to northern Protestants, the real obstacle to partition. In this period, though, republicans were far more concerned with the struggle against the Free State than with the North – even the Army Council found it necessary to remind its volunteers (who were 'inclined to ignore it') that 'Partition is one of the biggest and most important problems confronting the Nation.'[32]

Despite the contradictions of socialist republican ideology, Ryan was opposed to sectarianism and the influence of the Catholic Church. He had little difficulty in differentiating between his Catholicism and the political outlook of the hierarchy. He was a practising but somewhat ambivalent Catholic – he confided to Jacob, an enthusiastic agnostic, that he 'w[oul]d like to disbelieve in God but couldn't'. Ryan emphasised the necessity to separate republicanism from Catholicism: 'Sectarianism was one of the greatest curses. Unless it were eliminated, the struggle would not succeed. The struggle in which they were engaged was one between Republicanism and Imperialism; the religion – or even lack of religion – of the participants on either side did not matter.'[33] Of the annual republican pilgrimage to Bodenstown, Ryan forcibly remarked: 'We'll have no damn prayers here.'[34] He went against the popular tide in 1929 by writing a pamphlet critical of the Catholic Emancipation centenary celebrations and the role of O'Connell ('a master of an Orange Lodge' and 'Croppy hunter') in the 'mingling of religion and politics' and founding of constitutionalism ('the sorriest movement ever promoted in Ireland'). O'Connell 'was not the Liberator but the Enslaver' – 'the real Emancipators' were 'the physical force men'.[35] He had little time for the Free State's many craw-thumpers, describing the Catholic Truth Society as 'a rotten lot of chancers'.[36] At the same time, Ryan was not above emphasising his Catholicism as a means of combating clerical criticism, and his attacks on clerical influence were generally prefaced by protestations of his own religious orthodoxy.

But Ryan's growing stature in the IRA was based more on his activism than his political outlook. It was his skills as an agitator and propagandist that elevated him to an IRA leadership dominated by veterans of the War of Independence. An early protest – which 'built Frank's reputation' – was against the Abbey Theatre's showing of Seán O'Casey's *The Plough and the Stars* in 1926, which republicans viewed as an attack on the legacy of 1916.[37] Ryan organised republicans to disrupt its performances with smoke bombs and helped to organise a debate in which O'Casey broke down sobbing. Ryan's target was somewhat ironic given the play's theme. O'Casey, a socialist, juxtaposed the lofty ideals of the bourgeois separatists who led the Easter Rising with the grimy realities of alcoholism, prostitution and poverty in Dublin's slums. The idea that the revolution had been national but not social was a view with which Ryan agreed, but he never critically analysed the Rising or the ideology of its leaders. The riots also illustrated the intolerant mindset which existed among even socially progressive republicans. Ryan's activism frequently centred on the suppression of viewpoints at variance to his conception of republicanism; his adherence to 'the national faith' necessitated the suppression of non-believers such as ex-unionists and, worse still, Treatyite heretics.

The issue which really established Ryan within the IRA was his role in the protests against Armistice Day, the annual commemoration of the Great War. The Dublin parade, organised by the British Legion, involved as many as 20,000 ex-servicemen and 10,000 observers. Union Jacks and bunting were displayed outside the city-centre businesses and residences of wealthy Protestants, a visible symbol of the economically privileged position ex-unionists retained in the Free State. Armistice Day infuriated republicans, who viewed it as a provocative display of British imperialism. There was some truth to this: as well as commemorating the dead, the parades also functioned as an expression of unionist identity. The organisers regularly disobeyed the garda ban on military-style parades and display of Union Jacks, leading gardaí to complain that the Armistice parade 'was a definite Imperialistic display, and not a Commemoration to the War dead'. Their hostility to the event was also due to the fact that Armistice Day necessitated an enormous police operation and regularly brought chaos to the centre of Dublin. In 1928, for example, despite the large numbers of gardaí protecting a wide range of potential targets from cinemas to poppy depots, the IRA carried out synchronised bombings of three royal statues and brawls occurred throughout the day as poppy-wearers clashed with young republicans.[38]

Republicans, unsurprisingly, shared police scepticism about the commemorative aspect of Armistice Day but their arguments were more sophisticated than is sometimes allowed. *An Phoblacht* called for 'a really honest effort to collect men to commemorate comrades who were murdered in a callous, sordid struggle for world markets and Imperial expansion, but the emotion evoked to-day, while aroused by a call on comradely experiences and memories, is called to glorify the war itself, and the Empire that made it'.[39] However, it is evident from Ryan's speeches that intolerance of non-republican identity was also intrinsic. A central theme of *An Phoblacht* under Ryan's editorship was an obsessive desire to stamp out any public manifestation of non-republican identity. Rather than viewing ex-unionists as a wealthy but politically disempowered minority, they were presented as a threatening fifth column:

> They are actively, if in some districts quietly, organising all the anti-National and pro-British elements in the country. They have such organisations as the Legion of British Ex-Servicemen, Freemason Lodges, Baden Powell Scouts, Boys' Brigades, Girl Guides, British Fascisti . . . The Imperialistic menace is very real.[40]

Just as the parades functioned as a display of loyalty to Britain for many of their participants, the counter-demonstrations allowed for a show of republican strength and, along with Bodenstown, became one of the most important mobilisations in the republican calendar. Armistice Day provided for a rare show of republican unity, being the only annual occasion when the leaders of Sinn Féin, Fianna Fáil, the IRA and the communist movement shared a public platform. But the most potent aspect of Armistice Day was its symbolism: by forcing the government and police to defend poppy-wearers, republicans could depict the Free State administration as the defenders of British interests in Ireland. This was precisely the role which republicans attributed to Treatyites.

Ryan was a leader of the Anti-Imperialist League which organised the counter-demonstrations, but, as Jacob observed in 1926, he also played a part in the public disorder which invariably marked the occasion:

> I found poppy crowds standing in rows observing the silence, & other crowds walking or shouting. A few steps up the Green I perceived an ordered mob of young men marching in the roadway . . . and at their head Proinnsias & another, carrying a stick from which trailed a large Union Jack. The grave dignity of P., indulging in this childish sport, was impressive. They turned presently & marched down again, & then got involved with some peelers and between them & the peelers the flag was torn to bits . . . P. formed them up and gave them military orders as brazen as you please, with the help of that black cane that gives such an elegant finish to his appearance. The first Union Jack they found was out of the Church Representative Body house in Stephen's Green & it took them a while to deal with it but eventually someone got in & opened the door, and they went up & fetched it down & streeled it in the mud.[41]

Ryan's exertions were rewarded with dismissal from the Protestant-run Mountjoy School where he taught. His pugnacity was an important aspect of his appeal within the IRA. With his well-built six-foot frame, protruding ears and distinctive mop of black hair he was an easily recognisable figure and well suited to the demanding requirements of street politics. He was physically brave and enjoyed placing himself at the head of the brawling which accompanied republican protests. He seemed unfazed by the heavy beatings inflicted on him by poppy-wearers and the Special Branch (and by him on them). But increasingly, it was as an orator rather than brawler that Ryan made his mark on Armistice Day. He was one of the best speakers in Dublin although on paper his speeches do not appear particularly striking:

> Ireland was their Country and they would not allow the Union Jack to be shook in their faces. He invited the Police to stand aside and they would soon deal with Imperialism. They had put them from Leeson St to College Green, from there to the Park and the next place they would put them would be to the bogs. Argument should be met with argument and blow with blow.[42]

The speeches varied only slightly from year to year. The following year 'blow with blow' was replaced by 'bayonet with bayonet'.[43] But Ryan was one of the most passionate speakers in Dublin, and his speeches, always left to the end of the meeting, roused the crowd's enthusiasm. Some indication of his rhetorical style is given by Jacob's (admittedly biased) description in 1932:

> I never heard him so fierce . . . he got into 2 or 3 rages, and roared as if he must be heard to the far edge of the throng, which was *huge* (they had an amplifier) and he *has* a powerful voice. It seemed perfectly spontaneous, a sort of real battle fury that grew and burst, and it was nearly frightening to hear him. He seemed to swell up and get taller and broader. A lot about the men who died for the Republic too, and when are we going to have the pluck to come out again for it . . .[44]

Ryan's popularity was also partly due to the fact that he was invariably the most bloodthirsty speaker at any meeting. 'Imperialist blockheads', he declared, 'are not by nature susceptible to argument, they are susceptible to fear and must be made feel fear'.[45] At another meeting he declared: 'While we can use the arms which God has given us, no gunmen, uniformed or un-uniformed, will be suffered to interrupt us to-day.'[46] The recklessness of Ryan's seditious rhetoric invited arrest – indeed, he once complained 'how it hurt his dignity that [George] Gilmore should be arrested instead of him'.[47] When he was arrested in 1931, Dr Kathleen Lynn, a prominent republican, observed that 'he was always careless'.[48]

Ryan's role in Armistice Day raises questions about his ideological outlook. Some protests – poppy-snatching, smoke-bombing cinemas which played British war movies and the decapitation of royal statues – were harmless enough. But businesses, homes and, in several cases, families were attacked for displaying Union Jacks, and in 1929 a witness in a case against republicans who had seized a Union Jack was murdered.[49] That there was some contradiction between Ryan's non-sectarian journalism and his Armistice Day declarations such as 'Ireland for the Irish . . . Let those who want to honour their king get out to their proper country' seems evident.[50] Ryan seemed unaware of the discordance between the progressive rhetoric of republicanism and its day-to-day activism – aimed at such bastions of the 'garrison' as the Boy Scouts. Although convinced that a united republic would best serve Protestant interests, Ryan did not appear to see a connection between Protestants' lack of enthusiasm for unification and their treatment in the Free State. The inconsistencies were sometimes glaring. *An Phoblacht* urged the Free State authorities to emulate the North's treatment of Catholics: 'In the "six counties," if a man flies the Tricolour, the police at once order him to remove it . . . The official excuse is that it might "cause a disturbance". Well, the flying of Union Jacks in

Dublin will on all occasions "cause a disturbance"; so let the police take note and act accordingly. We are too damned tolerant.'[51] Ryan viewed the republican tradition as progressive because it would genuinely welcome Protestants as equals in a united Ireland, but to achieve this equality they had first to renounce their political and cultural allegiances. Protestants were entitled to equality, but only on republican terms.

But the limitations of Ryan's thinking must be understood in the context of his times – in the aftermath of the War of Independence and Civil War, the concept of tolerating conflicting political identities had negligible support on both sides of the border. Ryan's actions were extreme, but, by the standards of the prevailing nationalism, his sentiments were less so. Fianna Fáil opposed the display of Union Jacks and even the Garda Commissioner, Eoin O'Duffy, found the waving of Union Jacks (curiously by 'almost exclusively young girls') 'in the faces of citizens passing by in the course of their business' unacceptable.[52] Moreover Ryan, drawing a rigid if unrealistic distinction between religious and political affiliations, viewed the protests as anti-imperialist rather than sectarian. The Anti-Imperialist League which organised the protests, saw itself as (and organisationally formed part of) an international movement against imperialism.

In 1928 Ryan was writing travel brochures for the Irish Tourist Association, which employed several prominent republicans including Todd Andrews. In September he was arrested and charged with IRA membership when a police raid discovered documents in his desk. He refused to recognise the court and was placed in Mountjoy Prison when the jury failed to reach agreement. Considering what lay ahead of him, it was fortunate that Ryan could tolerate prison life:

Well, I guess folk are still passing votes of sympathy on me when they aren't cursing . . . At the moment, I'm just resuming old acquaintance-ships – from the Governor down to my fellow prisoners. I smoke while at exercise – I've piles of cigs. I read while I'm in . . . Would you believe it? – I seem to be gifted with far more patience than I gave myself credit for. I'm actually in good humour here, and I haven't found time being over heavy.[53]

He was returned to trial in February 1929, but fought the case, cross-examining Superintendent Ennis as to why no one had seen the police remove the documents from his desk and why they were not addressed to him. Neither fact was particularly surprising: IRA officers used false names for correspondence, and his col-leagues refused to testify against him. (Jacob was amused by Todd Andrews's account of 'Ennis's pained reproach at their lack of cooperation – "My God, Todd, didn't you see me take it out of the desk?"')[54] Ryan's speech to the jury was characteristic: 'It wasn't his business to prove his innocence, he was a Republican & didn't recognise the court or care a straw for the T[reason] A[ct] . . . it was the same treason for which Emmet, Mitchel, & the Fenians were tried in that court.'[55] He was acquitted but fired from the Tourist Association, whose owners resented the police attention. The Garda Commissioner, Eoin O'Duffy, was furious about the out-come, complaining about 'the spectacle of Judge Hanna, ex Black and Tan prosecutor . . . openly attacking the Garda'.[56]

Ryan's acquittal highlights the difficulties the police were facing in securing convictions for political crimes as civil law proved inade-quate to the IRA threat. It was difficult to select a jury that excluded every republican sympathiser or juror susceptible to intimidation. The garda, while initially popular owing to their non-political status, had lost support when Special Branch took over the army's role of policing subversives in 1925. They were not helped by

O'Duffy, who wished to put the element of force back into the police force. In 1926 he called for the arming of the Garda Síochána, arguing for 'aggression, real aggression, a practical authoritative interpretation of the badly misunderstood expression – Force . . . and the extermination of the type that is incapable, or unwilling to assume the responsibilities of citizenship'.[57] This was rejected by the Minister for Justice, Kevin O'Higgins, but his assassination by the IRA in the following year led Cumann na nGaedheal to intro-duce a draconian Public Safety Act. The IRA responded by inten-sifying its attack on the judicial system, targeting informers, witnesses, police and jurors. By 1929, conflict with the Special Branch had become the focus of IRA activism, and the police responded with the 'cat and mouse' policy – the constant arrest, release, and rearrest of known republicans. As O'Duffy explained, 'All one can do is hamper and hinder the movements of the criminals as much as is humanly possible; make them suffer, make their lives a burden, apply unremitting surveillance to their every movement and generally make their connection with conspiracy and murder a non-paying proposition.'[58] But coercion proved ineffective and arguably counter-productive, stiffening IRA resistance and diminishing public support for a police force that abused its powers and a government that increasingly eroded its citizens' constitutional rights.

Ryan was a prominent target of the crackdown, constantly watched, followed, searched and arrested. In the first two weeks of December 1929 he was arrested six times, an unpleasant process as described by an *An Phoblacht*: 'Two CID-men held his arms, twisting them. A third held him by the back of the neck, twisting his collar so as to choke him. A fourth kept punching him in the back.' (Although, in fairness, Ryan rarely left home without his cane which he swung at the heads of policemen to some effect.)[59] In February 1930 Ryan was acquitted of a series of dubious charges by Justice Little, who accused the police of abusing their powers, and the coercion campaign soon faltered as republicans proved adept at not only attacking but using the justice system. After a string of convictions of assault and compensation awards mounted against Special Branch the 'cat and mouse' policy was dropped. Ryan, however, was continually arrested throughout 1931 and even served a two-month spell of imprisonment after being beaten off a meeting platform by the police.

This attention was due both to Ryan's extremism and to his stature within the IRA. In 1926 he was appointed adjutant of the Dublin Brigade, the IRA's most important unit. By 1929 he was a salaried GHQ Staff Captain and member of the IRA executive. He was identified by the Garda Commissioner as a key figure in the 'small vicious gang' holding the IRA together: 'These men are still a nasty problem. They give their whole time and a great deal of energy to the fostering and cultivation of this dangerous secret society, travel about the country in motor cars, keep various units in touch, distribute war equipment and training instructions, and generally help to maintain the organization by the commission of acts of violence.' Ryan was particularly disliked for editing *An Phoblacht*: 'It openly advocates a doctrine of hate and violence against the Garda.' O'Duffy – describing Ryan as 'the murderer of D[etective] C[onstable] Sullivan' – commented: 'The young men who look upon him as a super patriot, and reading this doctrine, cannot be blamed if they consider it a duty to kill policemen.'[60] Ryan had few qualms about the use of violence. His notes for a lecture on the Invincibles (the secret society responsible for the 1882 Phoenix Park murders), seized by the police and circulated to the Executive Council, give an indication of his ruthlessness. Ryan lauded their idea of assassinating all holders of high office and blamed clerical and press propaganda for discrediting their legacy: 'This is no time for us to discuss the morality of war, the only question we can discuss is whether war would be of use . . . Catholics should know that there is authority from all Catholic teaching for killing tyrants.'[61] The implications of such rhetoric, shortly after the assassination of Kevin O'Higgins, were not lost on the government. There is no reason to believe Ryan did not mean what he said or, for that matter, organise and participate in the IRA's shocking killings, and it remains difficult to reconcile Ryan's warm persona with his extreme ruthlessness.

When O'Donnell ceased editing *An Phoblacht* in 1929, Ryan was his obvious replacement and proved extremely successful, at least until the IRA's left wing found itself out of step with the leadership in 1933. Under Ryan the emphasis tilted from socialism towards more traditional Pearsean rhetoric. The following editorial, with its militarism, spiritual rhetoric and slight downplaying of popular agitation, typified Ryan rather than O'Donnell:

As we believe with Pearse that Freedom can only be won in arms, we arrive at the logical conclusion that only an Ireland in arms can attain freedom . . . The Gaeltacht, Land Annuities, Unemployment, Irish-Ireland – these and a hundred other issues are but subsidiary problems. They take their origins from the British conquest of Ireland, and until that conquest is undone . . . not one of these other problems, important though they be, can find solution . . . We voice the sacred and inner urge that burns in the heart of every son and daughter of Ireland – however imposed ignorance or assimilated corruption may have dimmed its flame. We believe, too, that to our cause enemies and friends alike will apply the same simple test – they will judge that cause by the devotion which it inspires.[62]

Ryan's outlook echoed Pearse's militarism more than O'Donnell's Marxism: 'We want to see every man in Ireland trained to the use of arms, and in possession of those arms against England.'[63] He was also less enthusiastic about political methods, which he contrasted with 'the manly policy of Irish militant nationalism'.[64] Under Ryan's editorship *An Phoblacht's* circulation reportedly increased from around 8,000 to 40,000.[65] This was all the more impressive, considering the obstacles faced by Ryan. On many occasions, as *An Phoblacht* complained without much exaggeration, 'Every member of the staff was subjected to daily arrest, the paper was seized each week as it came off the machines, the offices of the paper and works in which it is printed and the private residences of the staff were beset and raided day and night.'[66]

Ryan's stint as editor was particularly significant, as it coincided with a period of left-wing radicalisation within the IRA. Despite O'Donnell's best efforts the IRA had remained socially conservative. O'Donnell's views had not reflected the leadership, and indeed irritated some of them, but in the late 1920s, much to the alarm of the government, police and hierarchy, a shift to the left occurred as the catastrophic impact of the Great Depression, which undermined capitalism and sent liberal democracies tumbling throughout Europe, impacted on the IRA's politics. In 1930 the IRA's chief of staff proposed a constitution calling for communal ownership of essential resources, and in the following year the IRA formally launched the avowedly socialist Saor Éire. Like all the IRA's political experiments in this period, it was a failure, but its consequences were significant. Confronted by an IRA which was both aggressively attacking the state and apparently communistic in outlook, the state resolved to crush the IRA. This necessitated removing the constitutional safeguards that had thwarted earlier attempts, a step which Cumann na nGaedheal felt required public backing from the bishops. Cosgrave assured them that a 'situation without parallel as a threat to the foundations of all authority has arisen' and handed over documents alleging an IRA conspiracy with Russian communism to overthrow the state.[67]

They were spiced with anti-clerical quotes from *An Phoblacht* and included an interview which Ryan had given to the *Daily Express* justifying a string of shocking IRA murders and threatening more. It was this interview that had originally led the Department of Justice to demand a new Public Safety Act. (De Valera felt it was simply an excuse to justify the bill, but complained that Ryan, if quoted accurately, had been 'acting the amadán'.)[68] Cosgrave's approach was effective. The hierarchy abhorred IRA violence, but saw it as a political rather than moral issue – particularly as clerical intervention against republicanism antagonised a substantial minority of the population. The threat to private property, however, proved more worrying than the occasional assassination. The hierarchy issued a collective pastoral which condemned the IRA's methods but focused its attack on Saor Éire, whose policies were described as 'a blasphemous denial of God and the overthrow of Christian civilisation'.

On 20 October Cosgrave introduced Article 2A, establishing a Military Tribunal with the power of death sentence and enacting other draconian measures. The police proclaimed the IRA and Saor Éire, *An Phoblacht* was suppressed, and the usual suspects were rounded up. The 'red scare' was successful in a narrow sense, but public disquiet at Cumann na nGaedheal's increasingly repressive methods was voiced. In political terms, the IRA probably benefited from the destabilising effects of republican violence and counter-repression. Peadar O'Donnell told Jacob that he found the new legislation 'most encouraging and he liked it'.[69] Ryan was arrested in December 1931 and brought before the Military Tribunal on charges of IRA membership. He refused to plead, but demanded 'a public inquiry into the conditions in Arbour Hill, where the Gilmores are being slowly done to death, and where convicted prisoners are treated like galley slaves, and where unconvicted prisoners are treated like criminals'.[70] Ryan was sentenced to join them for three months for contempt of court, after which he was to return to face the original charges. However, Ryan would not serve out his sentence, as the political climate was about to become utterly transformed.

CHAPTER 2

Socialist Republican, 1932–6

Ryan first suspected that Fianna Fáil had won the General Election the morning his warders neglected to throw him out of bed. The regime at Arbour Hill Military Prison had been tougher than Mountjoy; the prisoners were held in isolation and placed on bread-and-water diets on alternate three-day stretches. Ryan and Gilmore, who refused to wear prison uniforms or work, served part of their sentences in the unheated prison cells, naked except for towels, and on hunger strike.[1] The punishing regime ceased shortly after 16 February 1932 when it became evident that Fianna Fáil, with the support of Labour, had won enough support to form the next government. The first decision taken by the new Executive Council on 10 March was to release the prisoners. The ban on the IRA was lifted, and, for the first time since the Civil War, there were no political prisoners in the South.

Republicans greeted Fianna Fáil's victory with enthusiasm. *An Phoblacht* had supported de Valera, and IRA men worked on the ground to secure his victory. Fianna Fáil's campaign had incorporated IRA demands such as the withholding of annuity payments to Britain. But although Fianna Fáil's triumph might have been expected to revive the IRA's fortunes, the reality was quite the opposite; within four years the IRA was at its weakest point. With hindsight, its difficulties had been predictable, and astute republicans like Ryan had been under few illusions about the threat posed by

Fianna Fáil. The election of a government which claimed to be every bit as republican as the IRA and enjoyed a popular mandate would obviously pose more problems than Cumann nGaedheal. As Fianna Fáil shared the IRA's core aspirations, it became necessary for the IRA to define more precisely the objectives it stood for and how it expected to achieve them. These difficulties were heightened by Fianna Fáil's early successes. The rapid scrapping of the oath of fidelity, the retention of the annuities and a return to (economic) war with the 'old enemy' demonstrated that Fianna Fáil could implement a radical but constitutional republican agenda. Moreover, de Valera's conciliatory policies, such as the recruitment of republicans into the police and army, increasingly eroded the IRA's support base. Under these pressures, and its own internal tensions, the IRA began to unravel.

What was Ryan's response to Fianna Fáil's victory? An estimated 30,000 supporters attended the College Green rally to celebrate the release of the Arbour Hill prisoners. Ryan thanked Fianna Fáil for seeing 'that justice was done', but his speech must have caused concern. He began with some threatening remarks about 'the little Britishers – who were very quiet now and had to roll away their Union Jacks in moth balls'. He suggested they 'follow the example of Judas and take a rope', observing that 'they had been put out of public life and would never come back'. Although Fianna Fáil was secretly negotiating for the IRA's support, Ryan's speech was far from conciliatory: 'We're going to have a soft easy time for a while to come – maybe too soft and easy.' Their 'task was the achievement of an independent Irish Republic – whether they were persecuted or not they would have to continue that task'. His final comments, recorded by Special Branch, were a clear challenge to Fianna Fáil: 'Frank Ryan in the course of his speech asked the crowd did they want two Armies, and when the crowd shouted "No" he said, "Very well, we will have one army – the IRA."'[2]

His speech highlighted two issues that would create tensions between the IRA and the new government: the IRA's intention to pursue its own agenda, and its unwillingness to show magnanimity to the Treatyites. Ryan's stance echoed a recent article by his chief of staff, Moss Twomey, which had welcomed de Valera's proposals to 'chop off some of the Imperial tentacles' but emphasised the difference between this and the IRA's demand for a republic. Twomey pointed out that the IRA had helped to secure de Valera's election 'without hiding at all the fact that they believed the alternative administration offered the people could not lead them to re-establish the Republic and achieve their freedom'. He declared that 'the leadership of the Freedom Movement remains with the revolutionary movement' and demanded the coercion of 'bitterly anti-Irish organisations such as the British "Boy" Scouts . . . a powerful military organisation'.[3] The IRA's strategy was clear from an early point: it would harry Fianna Fáil into implementing a more radical agenda. This attempt to outflank Fianna Fáil represented a serious threat, as de Valera had secured power by a narrow margin which included both radical republicans and moderates, neither of which he could yet afford to alienate. But the IRA's major weakness was its uncertainty as to how to treat Fianna Fáil – as an ally, rival or enemy. Ryan, in the meantime, retired to Kilfenora to recuperate from his incarceration. Eilís described him as 'green in the face' and too weak to stand, while he confided to Jacob that he 'was in a bad way nervously'.[4]

These tensions became evident in the summer of 1932 when *An Phoblacht* embarked on a campaign for Eoin O'Duffy's dismissal and the disbanding of Special Branch which was widely backed by Fianna Fáil *cumainn*. It was soon widened to a call for all 'imperialist' forces – including the banks, big industries, Treatyite press and Cumann na nGaedheal – to 'be attacked and squelched. There must be no compromise with them, no tolerance for them, for there can be neither peace nor progress while they remain.'[5] Ryan's rhetoric was partly a response to Fianna Fáil's popularity which had placed the IRA on the back foot. As George Gilmore privately grumbled, 'Practically all the Republican and anti-FS feeling in the country is hopelessly pro–Dev.'[6] A revealing editorial indicates why 1932 marked the beginning of the end for the IRA in southern Ireland:

> But, when the Oath is removed, there will still remain the major task of asserting the sovereignty and unity of the Irish nation – ending Partition, ending the enforced foreign occupation of a portion of our territory and of our chief ports, ending, too, the conditions which make Acts of the elected representatives subject to the approval of Britain, through the Governor-Generals of Northern and Southern Ireland. Until these national humiliations are ended, it is idle to talk of discarding proven effective methods.[7]

With the exception of partition – for which Ryan, in an uncharacteristic moment of honest reflection, admitted 'We seem to have no remedy for'[8] – Fianna Fáil rapidly achieved these objectives. By 1938 de Valera had won a degree of sovereignty which the IRA could not have predicted possible. Such progress increasingly raised questions about the necessity for the IRA.

Once again commemoration provided the occasion for demonstrating tensions between the IRA and the state. Fianna Fáil had marched behind the IRA in the annual Bodenstown Parade as recently as 1931 and was now watched closely to see how it would act. Several weeks before the parade Ryan told Jacob that Fianna Fáil 'w[ould]n't go unless De V[alera] was to give the speech, & that was where the difficulty came'.[9] In the end Fianna Fáil adopted Cumann na nGaedheal's tactic of attending Bodenstown separately. Armistice Day provided a more heated occasion for fraternal tension, since Ryan and O'Donnell were radically escalating their campaign against the Treatyites. O'Donnell declared that 'every time the Cosgravian or any other imperialist party tried to hold a meeting in any part of the country . . . they would be pulled from the platforms'. Ryan characteristically put it more bluntly: 'No matter what anybody says to the contrary, while we have fists, hands and boots to use, and guns if necessary, there shall be no free speech for traitors.'[10] The following day Jacob met a predictably unrepentant Ryan: 'I said I heard he was to be indicted for his ferocious remarks . . . he said Like Hell I will.'[11] The 'No free speech for traitors' campaign, enthusiastically carried out by republican mobs throughout the state, was also a challenge to Fianna Fáil. Just as the IRA had forced Cumann na nGaedheal to protect ex-unionists, de Valera was compelled to choose between defending Treatyites or confronting republicans. The Department of Justice outlined the government's options in a memorandum to de Valera: first, to 'Let people say anything they like, so long, at least, as they are talking in an obviously rhetorical way to a mob', but 'if unhappily anybody is in fact murdered government will be charged with responsibility for the murder'. The alternative was to 'Exercise a strict supervision over such language . . . This means prosecution, trials before juries, imprisonment, hunger-strikes, and generally a reversion to the conditions which prevailed in recent years.' It would necessitate reviving Article 2A, and it would 'infuriate the IRA section' and 'expose the Government to the mockery of the Opposition ("We told you so")'. The memorandum concluded: 'My advice is to give the Ryans and O'Donnells a last warning . . . The Government has given these men every chance and every encouragement to behave themselves but they will not co-operate.'[12]

Ryan naturally chose not to behave himself, and *An Phoblacht*'s campaign escalated. He declared: 'There is only one effective answer to the Imperialist faction . . . "Squelch them". In no other country, in such a time of national crisis, would reactionary elements be allowed such liberty.' Ryan, no admirer of parliamentary democracy, complained that by allowing Treatyites to hold public meetings de Valera had 'substituted a false idea of democracy for National Sovereignty'. Fianna Fáil's protection of free speech was 'tolerance for treason'. Such thinking was not unusual among the republican left: George Gilmore, for example, told Jacob he 'was not for free speech all round, but only for it for deserving people like working class organisations'.[13] But the campaign proved counter-productive. In the short-term it provoked Treatyite counter-violence when the ex-servicemen's organisation, the Army Comrades Association, reorganised into a popular volunteer force pledged to protect Treatyite meetings. With the police, IRA, ACA and Fianna Fáil supporters involved in widespread street fighting, the winter of 1932 was one of the most violent since the end of the Civil War. Against this background, de Valera called a snap election which returned Fianna Fáil with an overall majority. *An Phoblacht* had supported de Valera – the alternative being unthinkable – but his election with an overall majority and a mandate for a more radical programme further weakened the IRA. Internal tensions, however, were to prove more destructive.

There had been a noticeable reluctance to resurrect Saor Éire after Fianna Fáil's election. A substantial section of the IRA opposed its communist flavour; some, while not hostile to socialism, felt it had undermined public support for the organisation, and others had always felt the army should not meddle in 'politics'. Ryan, who as editor of *An Phoblacht* exercised a key role in shaping the IRA's outlook, was among those increasingly unsatisfied with the IRA's lack of social radicalism. In October 1932 he fell out with Seán MacBride, the chairman of the Army Council, who had been recently appointed to 'act with the editor in controlling the policy of the paper', when MacBride attempted to exert influence over a

financial issue. Ryan reacted furiously, declaring that he had 'made
a paper out of a rag' and tendering his resignation. Underlying the
dispute was the Army Council's desire to reign in Ryan's independence. Ryan complained to Twomey that he had been relegated to
the position of a 'working editor' and was not taken into the Army
Council's confidence or allowed to influence editorial content.
(MacBride similarly complained that Ryan 'thinks he alone should
decide the policy of the paper'.) An army inquiry reached an uneasy
compromise which cannot have pleased Ryan. An advisory board
was established to maintain tighter control, but it was made clear
that the chief of staff 'is responsible for interpreting the policy
of the Army Council': 'The Editor (or any other volunteer) are
not personalities but instruments at the disposal of the organisation.'[14] Symbolically, Ryan's name no longer appeared under the
An Phoblacht banner on the editorial page from November 1932.
Ryan later complained that Twomey dictated his editorials in his
last months with *An Phoblacht*.[15]

   Ryan's discontent continued, and in February 1933 he tendered
his resignation in order to establish a weekly Irish-language newspaper. Ryan told Twomey: 'My heart is no longer in this paper',
somewhat tactlessly adding that he considered his new paper 'of
far more importance':

> Ever since '22, I've wanted to do it. Thinking things over in Arbour Hill
> I decided that if Cosgrave were driven out of power, there would not be
> a pressing need for me . . . I regret that I did not make this clear to you
> last October. Instead, I let minor points of difference arise with the
> result that there have been squabbles for which there was no real cause.[16]

Twomey's response was cool: 'What good will it do the IRA?'
Twomey, a respected and efficient chief of staff struggling to hold
the IRA together, was increasingly irritated by 'the little petty

things and organisations and groups' at work within the army.[17] MacBride more bluntly conveyed the Army Council's 'resentment at the waste of time incurred in investigating the fictitious grievances you put forward on so many occasions previously, as reasons for resigning'.[18] But Ryan's resignation should also be seen in the context of the IRA left's growing disillusionment. In the previous autumn George Gilmore had resigned from the executive on the grounds that he was 'completely fed up and pessimistic about everything past, present & future' (although, in contrast to O'Donnell, he did not believe that 'there is a revolutionary situation in the country only waiting for someone to assume leadership').[19] Ryan's resentment towards the leadership was evident from a blazing row with the IRA's adjutant general in March 1933. Ryan bitterly criticised the IRA's reluctance to support Jim Gralton, an Irish-born communist who was deported to the United States, accusing the army of 'being run by a secret clique'.[20] Disciplinary measures were avoided only after a formal apology.

These divisions were evident at the IRA convention in March 1933. Ryan supported O'Donnell's call for a return to Saor Éire, arguing that the alternative was to 'become a left wing of Fianna Fáil':

> I thought of the IRA in 1930–31 as a Citizen Army who knew what they wanted and were prepared to get it. It is strange that the programme that we decided on two years ago should meet with our indecision just now – it shows the defeatist spirit. How do our military men think that they can steer clear of politics?[21]

The call for a return to Saor Éire was defeated. Worse, the Army Council decided to put the left in its place. A resolution banning volunteers from joining other organisations or involving themselves in political agitation without permission was passed by a large majority, and a resolution expelling communists from the IRA (described by Ryan as 'sheer downright nonsense') was only narrowly defeated. Ryan retained his ruthless streak – his suggestion in the debate on the Special Branch was to 'have several objection-able people removed' – but strikingly Ryan, who had not been prominent in Saor Éire, was now one of the leading advocates of politicisation, largely in response to the new circumstances created by Fianna Fáil's election. From being a militarist with socially progressive inclinations he had become a leading spokesman of the IRA's left wing and made clear his dissatisfaction by refusing to allow his name to go forward for re-election to the executive.

Despite the disappointing convention Ryan reconsidered his resignation from *An Phoblacht*.[22] The Army Council, however, was intent on accepting it. Twomey complained to the assistant editor, Hanna Sheehy Skeffington: 'I sometimes wish myself, especially in the past year, that we had no paper. And candidly I do feel that many times Frank's attitude has not been too helpful. And in this paper there is more than journalistic attainments necessary in the Editor. To my mind the first essential is teamwork, and if this is absent no other qualifications could make up for that.'[23] Although Ryan's lack of co-operation with GHQ and poor relationship with his own staff were problems, genuine ideological differences were also central. Tellingly, Sheehy Skeffington, who had a strained working relationship with Ryan, resigned in the following week, citing much the same reasons: 'Now we seem to get cut-&-dry commands instead of an openly & freely discussed policy. We seem to be at a cross-road at present & while I see the need of caution & independence, it would be lamentable if your organisation were moving to the right, becoming a Bulmer-Hobson . . . wing of F[ianna] Fail.'[24]

Relations between the IRA left and the leadership deteriorated as anti-communism increased. One particularly divisive event was the burning of the communist-owned Connolly House in Great Strand Street in Dublin. On 27 March a hymn-singing mob ('God Bless Our Pope' and 'Hail Glorious St Patrick'), fired up by the belligerent sermons of the Lenten Missions, attacked the building, returning in greater numbers until they succeeded in burning it on 29 March. Charlie Gilmore was arrested for defending the house by the police (who had been less conspicuous during the rioting). To the disgust of the IRA left, Gilmore's claim in court that he had been authorised to carry his revolver was publicly denied by the adjutant general. Jacob noted Ryan's reaction: 'A. G.'s letter saying Charlie had no leave to have arms he said was "damnable" with great force.'[25] Ryan, O'Donnell and George Gilmore made a symbolic show of support by attending Charlie's trial (at which he was acquitted). There was some unease among the Dublin Brigade at the army leadership's treatment of Gilmore, but there was also a strong anti-communist element in the IRA. Many IRA men were devout Catholics who rejected the Church's criticism of the army but accepted its condemnation of communism. (In 1932 George Gilmore attributed the Dublin Brigade's poor showing in Bodenstown 'to the Retreat sermon that afternoon'.)[26] Many of the less devout were also anti-communist. Gilmore told Jacob he had been unable to round up volunteers to protect Connolly House, as they were both 'anti-religious & anti-com[munist] from want of thinking'.[27]

Ryan went on leave while Twomey decided where to transfer him. He travelled to France in May to see an osteopath, but was apparently arrested in Rennes after a statue was blown up.[28] He wanted a job that would leave him time to establish his newspaper and was in low spirits. He spent most of the summer walking from Dublin to Dingle, returning in September to take up the less sensitive position of Fianna organiser (where he helped train the next generation of republicans, including Cathal Goulding). Some sort of split now seemed inevitable. The IRA left was banned from speaking or writing on politics – 'A bloody awful position', O'Donnell complained – and Ryan fell out with the new IRA adjutant general, Donal O'Donoghue, when he was accused of attending the launch of the Communist Party.[29] Ryan refused to say whether or not he had been present unless 'properly charged – even on the evidence of a tout', adding that he 'would not regard membership of any Communist Party as a crime'. When Twomey intervened, instructing him to confirm or deny the report, Ryan revealed that he had not attended, adding: 'It hurts to think that I could be even suspected of deceit towards the organisation. If I found it impossible to submit to its discipline I would certainly notify you in advance.' Ryan's stubbornness had escalated a false report to the point of disciplinary charges, but his sense of grievance is understandable. By exaggerating the influence of the Communist Party, the IRA leadership alienated left republicans such as Gilmore and Ryan who were sceptical of the communists but had no desire to join in the witch-hunts.[30] The central figure in the closer alliance between the IRA left and the communist movement was actually Peadar O'Donnell, who may have been an 'underground' member of the Communist Party. He was certainly a 'fellow traveller' who organised communist cells within the IRA and promoted the party line at critical junctures.[31]

The IRA convention on 17 March 1934 provided the occasion for the split. As in 1933, the left attempted to persuade the IRA to commit itself to its radical social programme. They had won more support, including that of Michael Price, who had been prominent on the anti-communist side in 1933. O'Donnell and Gilmore's call for a 'Republican Congress' – essentially a revival of Saor Éire – was supported by Ryan:

Fianna Fáil who claimed that at one time alliance with us was of great value to them now . . . treat us with contempt. Seán MacBride wants a continuation of the present army activity – inactivity . . . He is afraid of leadership. What is wrong is a lack of decision. To prevent ourselves doing wrong we are all prepared to do nothing. This Convention could be a possible funeral of the IRA.[32]

The resolution was defeated by a small margin, and much of the IRA's left wing walked out. The split was confirmed by the launch of the Athlone manifesto on 8 April, which called for a broad front of anti-capitalist republican opinion. Workers, small farmers, the Gaeltacht youth and, rather optimistically, Ulster Protestant workers were identified as the movement's revolutionary basis. Republican Congress (the name officially adopted by the new organisation) has enjoyed favourable analysis, particularly from those who argue that it attempted to guide the republican movement from violent anti-democratic sectarianism towards a more progressive project. Certainly Congress emphasised that winning popular support for a radical programme was more important than militarism, an important and progressive ideological shift. Perhaps Congress's most significant advance was its attitude towards unionism:

Let us frankly admit that the Republican approach to the North has been, for years past, wrong. Republicans have adopted the attitude that the Protestant majority in the Six Counties are outside their world and the task for Republicans is to convert the Catholic minority to Republicanism . . . We put it to Republicans of all creeds, that their big task is to get the Protestant majority in the North-East to realise that the Republic is not a sectarian issue and their well-being is bound up with the freedom of unity of an Ireland ruled not by Catholic or Protestant capitalists, but by the Irish working class.[33]

Given the lack of enthusiasm for socialism among Irish nationalists and unionists, this was a programme with some limitations, but it represented a more sophisticated approach than that of the inter-war IRA. However, as Richard English's study has shown, simplistic perceptions of Congress have also served to exaggerate the extent to which it signified a shift from its violent anti-democratic roots.

Ryan asserted that Congress was not a turn to constitutional politics: 'Congress . . . would not be a step backward to constitutionalism; it would be a step forward to revolution.'[34] More explicitly he declared: 'No Republican now believes that the Republican Congress is a vote seeking party . . . Now, too, that the existence of the Irish Citizen Army is more generally known, Volunteers are not so much afraid that they will cease to become fighters if they participate in the Congress.'[35] This was no idle boast. Congress planned to conduct its struggle with political and military wings and began organising volunteers, mostly ex-IRA men, under the title of the 'Irish Citizen Army' (a shrewd stroke, given the original ICA's claim to the legacy of 1916). Unfortunately that ICA was still in existence, albeit as a sort of social club whose ageing membership attended commemorative functions. Its leadership was persuaded to accept Congress volunteers and was then pushed aside, although not without considerable acrimony.

The new ICA was reorganised on much the same basis as the IRA, with military training, regular parades and a GHQ exercising similar administrative procedures. Its constitution declared it 'the open armed expression of the struggle of the Irish Working Class for an Irish Workers' Republic . . . planned according to the principles laid down by James Connolly'. The constitution closely reflected Congress policy: 'The ICA believes that to attain its objects there will have to be a final appeal to the armed force. But in order to obtain the widest support of the people for its actions it advocates and supports any and every form of economic and political activity of the entire working class.'[36] The main distinction between the IRA and the ICA was the latter's more progressive policy of accepting women as volunteers and its intention to assassinate landlords and industrialists. However, as Paddy Byrne, the joint secretary of Republican Congress, recalled, with the exception of several botched operations, 'realistic political activity replaced militarism and it was decided to give the IRA their guns back'.[37] The ICA had been partly symbolic – an attempt to show that socialism was as manly as republicanism – but its failure was also due to Congress's subsequent split (in September 1934) which rendered it irrelevant.[38]

That Congress did not exactly mark a decisive turn from violence can also be seen from its attitude to the Blueshirts. One reason for the IRA split had been the left's insistence that the Blueshirts were a fascist threat to be met with force. The IRA leadership more astutely viewed them as a distraction and feared that IRA–Blueshirt violence would enable de Valera to suppress both. The difference between the attitudes of Congress and the IRA on this question in the summer of 1934 was striking. While *An Phoblacht* repeatedly called for republicans to show restraint, *Republican Congress* demanded they 'squelch the Fascist menace'.[39] There has been far less criticism of the anti-fascist campaign of 1934 than the 1932 campaign to 'squelch the Traitors'. Violence against fascists is quite a different thing to the suppression of a defeated opposition. Many European socialists would have agreed with Congress's warning:

Fascist meetings are demonstrations of strength organised to concentrate Fascist forces at selected points. These meetings are intended primarily to terrorise. Blueshirts are gathered in from far-away centres, equipped with batons, knuckle-dusters and stray revolvers. The assembly is then to spread terror through the district so that the local Fascist

branch may appear a formidable force, backed by an irresistible might . . .
Every successful Fascist rally is a step forward to the Fascist dictatorship.[40]

With their shirts, raised-arm salute and belligerent proclivities,
the Blueshirts managed a reasonable imitation of European fascist
movements. There were also elements among the leadership,
notably Eoin O'Duffy, who wished to establish a fascist dictatorship. But the similarities between the 1932 and 1934 campaigns
seem greater than the differences. Both were provoked by the
insistence of the IRA left – Ryan, in particular – that their opponents
did not have a right to free speech. Just as he accused England of
backing the 'traitor menace' in 1932, Ryan claimed England was
behind 'the Fascist menace'. It was also essentially the same people
involved in the brawls in places such as Tralee – few of who would
have identified themselves as 'traitors' and 'anti-imperialists' in
1932 or 'fascists' and 'anti-fascists' in 1934. The main difference
was that the Treatyites lashed back in 1934. What was really
behind Congress's campaign was an attempt to outflank Fianna
Fáil and the IRA by placing itself at the head of the widespread
violence (which was in reality a product of Civil War bitterness and
rural anger about the Economic War, brought about by de Valera's
withholding of land annuity payments to Britain). This agenda is
evident from Ryan's unsubtle editorials: 'The masses of the Irish
people are passionately anti-Fascist and only await the call to rally.
But they have been flatly deserted. Fianna Fáil asks them in effect
to allow Fascism entrench itself under the protection of police and
soldiers. The controlling body of the IRA shirks leadership.'[41] In
the short term it was perhaps astute to attempt to win over the considerable numbers of republicans keen to engage in such conflict,
but the strategy failed. Congress lacked sufficient strength to place
itself with any credibility at the head of the agitation; rather than
leading the masses, there were 'as many Congress leaders as fol-

lowers'.[42] It was also an attempt to place an ideological significance on the conflict that did not exist – the republican mobs that attacked O'Duffy were anti-Treaty, not anti-fascist. The implosion of the Blueshirts in late 1934 left Congress as an anti-fascist movement without a fascist menace.

The relationship between Congress and the IRA was unsurprisingly poor. The IRA had expelled the left-wing dissidents and taken the high moral ground against 'their criminal and senseless disruptionist campaign'.[43] Fraternal tensions were played out at Bodenstown. One notorious event invariably recalled to illustrate the sectarian nature of the IRA was the attack on Congress supporters, including a Protestant delegation from the Shankill, at Bodenstown in 1934. Peter O'Connor's account is indicative: 'An incident occurred there which caused me and several of my comrades to leave the IRA for good. A group of Protestant working-class lads from the Shankill Road, Belfast . . . were attacked and prevented from laying a wreath on the grave of Wolfe Tone by a section of the IRA.'[44] Another account depicts the attack as a turning point in the fortunes of Congress 'which had begun to attract broad working-class support on both sides of the border'.[45]

But the issue was less clear cut. Bodenstown, the most important republican demonstration, was controlled by the IRA under the auspices of the Wolfe Tone Commemoration Committee. This body had warned Congress that only banners for which permission had been given (those of groups that recognised the IRA's authority) could be carried in the parade from Sallins. Before the march Congress conceded: 'The parade is under IRA auspices. Therefore the regulations will be observed by us.'[46] But on the day itself Congress refused to furl its banners before the parade. Both sides were to disagree about what followed. *An Phoblacht* reported that when Congress attempted to break through their stewards, their banners were seized, although not that of the Belfast group, as 'they, unlike others, did not come here for the purpose of causing trouble'.[47] Congress preferred to emphasise the attack against the Belfast contingent in a rather self-righteous editorial entitled 'A Day of Shame': 'We could not submit to a regulation that would have us suppress ourselves. We insisted on our right to carry our banners . . . The lesson of the Bodenstown fight is that the working of the Congress must now be pushed within the IRA units with renewed energy.'[48] Whatever the exact circumstances, it is difficult not to attribute much of the blame to Congress, who appeared intent on provoking a reaction from the IRA. For some within Congress, and historians sympathetic to its outlook, this incident would subsequently provide a convenient explanation for Congress's lack of success in the North.

Republicans who had initially sympathised with Congress were now forced to choose sides. Cumann na mBan's Eithne Coyle and Sighle Humphreys resigned from Congress because they believed its 'main objective . . . was to smash the Irish Republican Army and *An Phoblacht*'.[49] They claimed that Ryan 'said that his chief aim as editor of *The Republican Congress* was to expose the hypocrisy and dishonesty of *An Phoblacht*'. They complained also about the decision to create an armed force, as the alleged reason for the split had been 'that in concentrating on military training the IRA was neglecting the more important revolutionary work'. They added: 'We cannot see our way to remain on a Committee which has not the moral courage to say that Connolly's philosophy and social principles are more suited to the Irish people than the foreign pagan and materialist philosophy which so many insinuate is the only solution to the capitalist state of society.' These criticisms appear for the most part convincing, but even those which are not, such as their apparent ignorance of James Connolly's Marxism, illustrate the ideological confusion which doomed Congress from the beginning. Congress included an uneasy combination of radical republicans, socialists and communists. Nostalgic recollections of Congress as an oasis of progressive thought should be balanced against the obvious approval of some of its leaders for the Stalinist model: Roddy Connolly made it clear that Congress would 'liquidate' the 'remnants and forms of other classes' until the Workers' Republic was achieved.[50] One *Republican Congress* editorial noted: 'Ranchers and big farmers, Ireland's Kulak class, are a comparatively small section of the Irish population . . . In the wars for Irish Independence they were the enemies of the revolution. Unfortunately, they were allowed survive.'[51] Ryan's rhetoric became noticeably more Marxist in 1934, his prose dotted with allusions to 'revolutionary vanguards', but this probably reflected the editorial line rather than a conversion to Marxism. He was an activist rather than a theorist, and his biographer is probably right to suggest that 'Ryan took his cue from O'Donnell and Gilmore' in such matters.[52] Ryan's political vision was a fairly uncomplicated fusion of republicanism and socialism: 'The future lies in working–class rule. In my opinion, not in the Communism advocated today, but certainly in that direction . . . Eventually the gap between the CP policy on the one hand and the Fianna Fáil and IRA policies on the other hand will be filled by a new movement.'[53]

Congress's lack of ideological coherence was exposed at the September 1934 conference, when a deep split destroyed the movement as a political force (although its first six months hardly promised a bright future). The Rathmines conference divided on the question of whether to establish a new party advocating a Workers' Republic (Michael Price, Roddy Connolly) or a looser united front supporting an Irish Republic (O'Donnell, Ryan and Gilmore). Essentially the question was: what type of organisational structure was most suitable, and to what extent should the emphasis be placed on socialism rather than republicanism? O'Donnell's speech typified the lack of ideological clarity within Congress. He argued that the Workers' Republic was too radical: 'Wasn't it clear that what most people wanted to see in their day was the establishment of an Irish Republic? Here, then, in the permanent and universal sentiment of nationalism was a force that should be and could be turned to account. Establish a Republic in Ireland, said Peadar O'Donnell and 24 hours later you will have in fact a Workers' Republic.'[54] But if this was the case, why had O'Donnell and Ryan broken from the IRA? They had long claimed that the IRA's mistake had been to put nationalism before socialism. Congress's founding Athlone manifesto had begun with James Connolly's dictum that a Republic could 'never be achieved except through a struggle which uproots capitalism on its way'. And how likely was the 'universal sentiment of nationalism' to attract Protestant workers? In reality, O'Donnell's faction had executed a massive ideological U-turn between Athlone and the conference, and were now advocating the 'stages theory' – the communist idea that a bourgeois nationalist state (the Irish Republic) must precede a socialist one (the Workers' Republic). It seems likely that the CPI, which was influential within Congress, had persuaded (or instructed) O'Donnell to support the less radical motion which tallied with Soviet policy. Price and around half the Congress walked out. The remaining activists and the CPI become increasingly interchangeable in terms of membership and policy.

Rathmines resulted in a wave of splits reminiscent of Monty Python's 'People's Front of Judea'. Price's faction withdrew from Congress to fight their ground within the ICA where Special Branch's infiltration of the Kilkenny branch revealed the full extent of the confusion. Three ICA GHQs (O'Donnell–Ryan, Price–Connolly, and the original leadership) claimed the loyalties of the bewildered 15-member branch, sending streams of orders, countermanding orders, expulsion notices and virulent newsletters to its members, who had little understanding of the disputes or personalities involved. By November Price had broken with the Connolly faction – essentially comprising the siblings Nora and Roddy – who themselves promptly split, Roddy preserving Nora's newsletters to amuse workers in the Revolutionary Museum to be built in the Worker's Republic.[55] The splits (as Brendan Behan observed, always the first item on the agenda of a republican meeting) demonstrated the contrast between the aspirations of radical republicans and their utter inability to achieve agreement on a basic programme. Ryan was as much at fault as anyone, complaining bitterly of his rivals: 'Three or four "Republican parties" spending their time fighting each other, each insisting that it alone will get the Republic; it's tragic. The people want unity; the leaders thwart them.'[56] This recurring problem within radical republicanism has been attributed to the political culture of its advocates; the very aspects of Ryan's outlook which sustained his radicalism in the face of opposition and apathy – his belief that his programme, even as it changed from month to month, was the only viable one, his exclusive identification of his beliefs with those of 'the people', and his intolerance of political opposition contributed to his failure to build an effective party.[57]

The following year, 1935, was not destined to witness any revival in Congress's flagging fortunes. Whereas Congress had begun by organising rent strikes, campaigning against slum landlords and generally taking the offensive on a wide front of issues, its activism became increasingly defensive. Ryan spent much of early 1935 campaigning for the reinstatement of Frank Edwards, who had been fired from his teaching post by the Bishop of Waterford for supporting Congress. Bodenstown, as Jacob recorded, witnessed much the same scenes as the previous year despite the fact that Congress only mustered 40 members:

We were marshalled in order, a good lot, but all the women put at the back – for safety according to George [Gilmore] – till Cora H[ughes] came along & protested, after which we were put in the middle . . . last but for the Communists who had a big red flag with Connolly's portrait on it but not their name. As we came into the 1st field with P[roinnsias] & another stalwart carrying our name-banner in front, it and they were attacked by a detachment of IRA men stationed there to do it, & there was a bit of a fight, the banner was torn in 2 & I saw P. laying about with the stick attached to half of it, & George very active too – a general fight with sticks & a stout red man roaring 'Fall in Westmeath!' – after a bit of confusion we were marching out of the fields onto the road with the torn banner and the cheers of the spectators.[58]

Compared with the crowds which Ryan had once addressed, Congress attracted insignificant numbers. As Special Branch reported on the May Day celebration, 'Not more than 100 marched in the procession and not more than 250 were present . . . The general public took absolutely no interest.'[59] Ryan, off the IRA payroll since the split, struggled to make a living from the Co-Operative Press. As well as producing *Republican Congress* without much help, Ryan handled the machines and the business – a 16-hour day which took a toll on his health. In early 1936 he was hospitalised with heart trouble and was warned that without regular rest and less drinking and smoking his health would deteriorate.[60] In early 1936 *Republican Congress* finally folded.

The events of Easter weekend were a further blow for Republican Congress. When Congress and CPI members attempted to join a march to Glasnevin, they were attacked and beaten by Blueshirt onlookers and some of the other republican contingents.[61] The following day they attempted to hold a public meeting. Given the revival of anti-communism, the decision to invite Willie Gallacher, a British Communist MP (for which Ryan blamed the

CPI) was tactically dubious.[62] Special Branch reported that 'about 98%' of the 5,000-strong crowd came to disrupt the meeting. Police protection saved the speakers from assault, but a hail of missiles, including razor-blade-embedded potatoes, broke it up. O'Donnell was amused by the 'hostile peeler' in front of him who bore the brunt of the bombardment: 'Ye poor bastard', he told the unfortunate garda, 'it's bad enough to suffer for a thing you believe in but it's hard luck being knocked about for what you object to'.[63]

But the plight of Congress was more serious. After the meeting an anti-communist mob rampaged through the city attacking the Congress office, CPI headquarters and less pertinent targets such as Trinity College. Ryan now admitted that 'Congress – from an organisational point of view – is only a name.'[64] To the amusement of his Treatyite opponents, he organised a campaign to protest the denial of free speech to Congress. Ryan complained that the attacks were due to 'religious bigotry working on the crowd', which to some extent they were, but there was no disputing Congress's unpopularity. Ryan polled just over 1 per cent of the vote in North-East Dublin in the local elections in June, the expense of which bankrupted the Co-Op Press. By the summer of 1936, Republican Congress had collapsed. But, just at a time when it seemed that Ryan was left without a viable political role, he was to become swept up in the political forces that were beginning to tear Europe apart.

CHAPTER 3

Anti-fascist, 1936-8

The Spanish Civil War began on 17 July 1936 when a group of right-wing military officers launched a coup against the democratically elected Popular Front Government. It divided the left (socialists, republicans, Republican Left, anarchists and communists) from the right (Catholic conservatives, monarchists and the fascist Falange). Underlying this alignment were deep-rooted social divisions between 'old Spain' – the army, Catholic Church, landowners and wealthy – and the landless labourers, trade unionists and progressive middle-class of Republican Spain. When Italy and Germany lent support to the Nationalists, and the Soviet Union backed the Republic, it became apparent that Spain could start a second world war. In response, Britain and France secured general international agreement for non-intervention – a policy of holding the ring while the Spanish resolved the conflict. It proved ineffective and morally dubious, preventing Spain's legal government from purchasing arms while the fascist powers, and to a lesser extent the Soviet Union, flagrantly breached the agreement.

For many radicals, Spain polarised the bitter social and ideological divisions of inter-war Europe into a clear choice – the left or the right, Franco or the Republic. In Ireland, as in most countries, the complexities of the war were lost on most observers. The most striking aspect of the Irish response was the immense outpouring of public support for Franco's Nationalists in the summer of 1936.

The catalyst for this was the sensational newspaper reports of atrocities committed against priests and nuns in Republican territory which sparked a 'red scare' more intense than those of the early 1930s. The pro-Franco Irish Christian Front attracted huge crowds in mass rallies throughout the country, while trade unions and branches of the main parties passed pro-Nationalist resolutions. Few foreign issues of the twentieth century provoked the same level of discussion, outrage and enthusiasm as the Spanish Civil War – a response which must be understood in the context of the intense self-conscious Catholicism of 1930s Ireland. Despite the overwhelming degree of pro-Franco support, the Irish far left were as enthusiastic about the Spanish Republic as other European socialists. Indeed, the manner in which the republican left's old enemies – the hierarchy, the Blueshirts and the *Irish Independent* – lined up behind Franco strengthened its commitment to the cause. Rosamond Jacob's diary vividly conveys the urgency with which left republicans discussed Spain that summer. But it was not apparent how their support could be demonstrated. The Christian Front's campaign had revived anti-communism and attempts to hold pro-Republic meetings were broken up by mobs. The question of military support for the Republic was raised as the Comintern (the Soviet-controlled communist parties) was recruiting volunteers for the International Brigades, but Congress opposed the idea; on 17 September Ryan told a friend: 'I wouldn't go to Spain . . . I feel I have to stand my ground here and rally our own. The frontline trenches of Spain are right here.'[1] Within two months Ryan was leading the first contingent of Irishmen to join the International Brigades. Why did he change his mind?

The reason probably lies in a combination of the political and the personal. On 16 September 1936 Congress issued a telegram of support to the Spanish government. In response, Cardinal MacRory, the Primate of All Ireland, urged the Irish government to suppress

Congress and declared it 'a scandal and an outrage that an Irish
Catholic [*sic*] body' should support 'a movement that seeks to
destroy faith in God, faith in Jesus Christ, and faith in the world to
come, and that is pledged also to destroy every Christian State in the
world'.[2] MacRory's outburst, which heralded a clerical campaign of
support for Franco, provides an indication of the intellectual level of
the discussion on Spain. Ryan, not one to meekly accept a rap from
the crozier, responded with an open letter in defence of the Spanish
Republic which demonstrated his considerable abilities as a polemi-
cist. He linked the bishops' and O'Duffy's support for Franco with
their pro-Treaty stance in 1922 and stressed the republican (in both
the Irish and Spanish sense) rather than socialist significance of the
conflict. He compared the Spanish atrocity stories with the (then)
discredited British propaganda about 'Catholic Belgium' in 1914
and drew attention to the Nationalist massacre of 2,000 Catholics at
Badajoz. He questioned the credentials of the 'Mohommedan
Moors' and 'godless scum of the foreign legion' to represent the
forces of Christianity, ending with the declaration:

> We Republicans deny that religion is at stake in Spain just as we
> denied – in the teeth of ecclesiastical condemnation – that religion was
> at stake when we were fighting in arms to defeat the Cosgrave
> Government in 1922–23. Our stand in 1922–23 is already vindicated:
> history will vindicate our stand on the Spanish question to-day.[3]

The attempt to present the Spanish Civil War in an Irish historical
context was tendentious but shrewd, particularly if support was to
be mobilised from the wider republican movement. But it met with
limited success; in a conflict widely presented as one between
Christianity and communism there was no doubt where nationalist
Ireland's support would reside. But, regardless of its effectiveness,
the controversy strengthened Ryan's commitment to Spain.

Less tangible political factors – anti-fascism, internationalism and the symbolic importance of Spain – were also important. These motives were reflected in Ryan's statement when the first contingent left for Spain:

> It is a demonstration of the sympathy of revolutionary Ireland with the Spanish people in their fight against international Fascism. It is also a reply to the intervention of Irish Fascism in the war against the Spanish Republic which, if unchallenged, would remain a disgrace on our own people. We want to show that there is a close bond between the democracies of Ireland and Spain.[4]

The reference to democracy, not a sentiment previously associated with Ryan, was both tactically astute and reflected the Comintern line, which presented Spain as a conflict between democracy and fascism rather than left and right. But the critical motives for Ryan were rooted in Irish rather than international factors, and the decision of Eoin O'Duffy to lead a force of Irishmen to fight for Franco was central. This was a provocation which Ryan was unable to ignore, as he later made clear in a letter from a Spanish jail: 'I didn't bring a batt[alio]n to Spain. I could have done so. In fact, I prevented many from coming. I was satisfied with just enough to offset the O'Duffy propaganda.'[5] Spain revived both the moribund far right and left, providing them with a politically significant role, albeit one that had to be played out on a foreign stage.

The political motives are evident, but what of personal ones? This remains a contentious issue in the historiography of the International Brigades. Left-wing historians tend to stress idealistic political motives over personal ones: volunteers are often presented as selfless representatives of whatever cause Spain is taken to signify, be it communism, anti-fascism or the defence of liberal democracy. Such historians agree that the previous experiences of volunteers – such as anti-fascist or trade union activism – are crucial, but place less emphasis on the importance of the individual's specific circumstances. In contrast, Hugh Thomas has observed that many of the volunteers from Britain 'desired some outlet through which to purge some private grief or maladjustment'. However, Valentine Cunningham's observation that a 'convergence of personal and public crisis' led many to Spain may provide a more rounded insight into Ryan's decision.[6] The public crisis was the failure of Republican Congress and, for the time being, the left republican project in Ireland. This was also a personal crisis, leaving Ryan without a political role or even a job. (Jacob noted George Gilmore's criticism of Ryan around this time: 'G. talking severely about P., thinks he sh[oul]d look for a job, sub-editor in paper, for instance').[7] Ryan also liked a fight; viewing violence as a sign of commitment and belief in a cause. It seems likely that a combination of the virulence of the pro-Franco campaign, political factors and personal circumstances influenced Ryan.

He left on 11 December 1936 without telling his family or many close friends. Eilís raced to Westland Row station when she heard he was leaving: 'Frank got out of the carriage when he saw me and he walked away down the platform. He put rosary beads into my hand and said, "Tell mother and father that I'm not a 'red'. I am going to fight for democracy in Spain."'[8] Ryan's group of 80 volunteers, composed of communists, IRA men and Congress members, travelled to France by train and crossed the Pyrenees on foot. An account of their eventful arrival in Figueras on 15 December illustrates both the tensions there and Ryan's leadership qualities. A drunken Irish communist had fired a shot in the middle of the night, and the Irishmen were woken by guards at gunpoint. 'Ryan took in the situation in an instant', reported one of those present, 'and shouted orders that none was to interfere. Ryan said that the prisoner, the worse for wine, was disgracing us all. Shouting in

French, Ryan tried to tell the Catalan guards that they had our support.' The volunteers were addressed by an officer whose attire bore an unfortunate resemblance to that of the Blueshirts:

> He was very pleased that his guards had apprehended one of the agents sent in by the reactionaries to disrupt and destroy the Republican Army . . . He was sure that we would be glad to know that this unknown mystery man would face a court-martial, and execution. [Dave] Springhall pushed a Londoner named Stone to the fore to translate in the shouting match that had developed between Ryan and the Commandante. Youthful Dubliners regarding what was going on as an amusing mistake began to shout 'release the pri-son-er'. They mimicked the shrill voices of 'Madam [MacBride]'s Auld-ones' . . .[9]

The Irishman was released when the commandant grasped the situation. It was an amusing incident, characteristic of the comparatively irreverent outlook of the Irish in Spain, but it was also an introduction to the chaotic factional atmosphere of Republican Spain and encapsulated Ryan's primary role there – to liaise between the authorities and the Irish and protect his men whenever possible.

Ryan's group arrived in Madrigueras training base soon afterwards. On 23 December, with little training, an Irish unit of 43 men was loaned to the Franco–Belgian battalion on the Cordoba front. (Within four days eight were dead, an early indication of the scale of casualties within the International Brigades.) The reaction of Joe Monks to this unit's formation is interesting: 'To our amazement "Kit" Conway instead of Frank Ryan had been appointed Section Commander . . . Frank Ryan brought his speech to an end with the astonishing statement that he was not coming to the front with us. There were matters that had to be taken care of in respect of the position of the Irish in the envisaged 16th

Battalion.'[10] Ryan was preoccupied with other problems, but Monks's surprise raises the curious point that Ryan never held a field command position in Spain. He had told his parents that his deafness meant he would be involved in propaganda rather than fighting.[11] But while Ryan was of most use to the Republic in this capacity, there was probably more to his backstage role. The sincerity of his letter to his parents can be questioned, as Ryan rarely let his parents know when he was in trouble. Nor was he was the type to recruit inexperienced young men while he worked in safety behind the lines (as was borne out by his subsequent actions). It seems likely that Ryan was prevented or dissuaded from leading his men, the most likely reason being the influence of the Communist Party. Despite the Brigades' formal anti-fascist unity and the heterogeneous background of its volunteers, the Communist Party maintained a tight grip over every aspect of the International Brigades. As James Hopkins has observed, 'For those who had "military ambitions" in the war, the party was the sole route to positions of higher command and responsibility.' The non-communist George Nathan, for example, 'who had brilliantly commanded the famed No. 1 Company, [and] was the logical person to take charge of the British Battalion' was assigned to a position on the 15th Brigade staff. Ryan, presumably for the same reason, also ended up on the brigade staff.

Ryan's more immediate problem was the deployment of the hundred Irishmen training in Madrigueras alongside several hundred British volunteers. He was unable to convince the brigade command to sanction a separate Irish unit, given their insufficient numbers and the obvious military logic of organising soldiers in language-based battalions. On 1 January 1937 Ryan sent a circular to his men appealing for patience: 'The closest bonds of comradeship must unite us with all the fighters against Fascism from other countries. Rival national war-cries will never be raised by us.'[12]

Nonetheless, serious difficulties between the Irish and British led a small majority of the Irish volunteers to refuse to fight in the 'British battalion'. National differences had been exacerbated by the presence of George Nathan, an ex-Black and Tan (and murderer of the mayor of Limerick in 1921) and the jingoistic attitude of the early British officers, whom Ryan described as 'the swelled-headed adventurer type'.[13]

The split, reminiscent of the earlier Congress one, divided the internationalists from the more nationalist-minded volunteers, who decamped to the nearby American base (after a mutinous show of force).[14] When Ryan returned from Madrid, he found several of his men under arrest and the remainder split between two units. He maintained that 'the representatives of the British CP wrecked the Irish unit', in particular the battalion commander, Wilfred Macartney (who had also lost the confidence of his British officers).[15] His anger was evident at a Burns night celebration held just before the British battalion headed to the Jarama front. Peter Kerrigan, a political commissar, recalled:

> Frank got up near the end of the celebration and he made a speech . . . to request that the Irish in the battalion should be transferred immediately from the English [*sic*] battalion to the American Lincoln-Washingtons who were not yet up to the front. Well, this was rather devastating, we were on the eve of going into action. And Marty, André Marty blew his top. Immediately ordered two men to fall in and arrested Ryan on the spot and it took the combined efforts of myself, [Tom] Wintringham and Springhall to finally succeed in getting Ryan released.[16]

Ryan had made a powerful enemy in Marty – 'the oddly ridiculous and thoroughly murderous head of the International Brigades' – who directed a ruthless ideological regime within the brigades.[17]

But serious as these problems were, they did not cast much of a shadow over the military efficiency of the British battalion, which earned a reputation for valour.

On 12 February the 600-strong British battalion (including Ryan, who liaised between the battalion and brigade staff) moved up to the Jarama front into what was expected to be a reserve position behind a Republican advance. In fact the Nationalists had launched a massive attack which had overrun the Republican forward units. Three battalions of the 15th Brigade, comprising the main military presence in the exposed southern sector of the front line, took up positions near the village of Morata de Tajuna and within hours encountered one of the most savage onslaughts of the war. Paul Preston has described the month-long Jarama battle which killed around 17,000 soldiers as 'the most vicious fighting of the entire Civil War'.[18] Yet that afternoon the 15th Brigade, a multinational army of revolutionaries many of whom had never fired a gun in combat, held off Franco's elite troops – a feat described by one military historian as 'among the most impressive achievements of modern warfare'.[19] But the price was appalling. By the end of its first day in action the majority of the British battalion were wounded or dead. The capture of the machine-gun company on the following day further weakened it, and by the third day 200 survivors were barely hanging on. With most of their officers dead, and under heavy fire, isolated sections of the British battalion began to retreat in disarray. General Gal, the 'incompetent, bad-tempered, and hated' 15th Brigade commander, aware that the front had momentarily collapsed, ordered them to return to their position.[20]

The reason for Gal's concern, and the ferocity of Jarama, was the strategic importance of the Madrid-Valencia road. The Nationalist attack hinged on capturing the road; if it fell, in all likelihood, so too would Madrid. It was at this critical point that

Ryan made a genuinely heroic contribution which reversed the rout on that section of the line. As Joe Monks recalled, 'Ryan and [Jock] Cunningham actually led the march back to the line. Each time that Ryan shouted to the marching ranks: "Are we downhearted?" a forest of clenched fists was raised as, unafraid, the men answered with a resounding "No!"'[21] Ryan had little military experience, but understood morale, as he later recounted:

> The crowd behind us was marching silently. The thoughts in their minds could not be inspiring ones. I remembered a trick of the old days when we were holding banned demonstrations. I jerked my head back: 'Sing up, ye sons of guns.'
>
> > Then comrades, come rally,
> > And the last fight let us face;
> > The Internationale
> > Unites the human race.
>
> On we marched, back up the road, nearer and near to the front. Stragglers still in retreat down the slopes stopped in amazement, changed direction and ran to join us; men lying exhausted on the roadside jumped up, cheered and joined the ranks. I looked back. Beneath the forest of upraised fists, what a strange band! Unshaven, unkempt, blood-stained, grimy. But full of fight again, and marching on the road back.[22]

Hearing the singing, their exhausted attackers assumed reinforcements had arrived and pulled back, enabling the battalion to reoccupy its original position and secure the Madrid-Valencia road. But, as Ryan could not but notice, the front remained active the following day:

> I got a slight flesh-wound in the arm from a bullet that went through the head of a man beside me . . . Half an hour later, a tank shell burst

beside me and I got a wallop in the left leg that knocked me down . . . I got a bullet through the left arm. It's a clean wound, high up and will be OK in a few weeks more.[23]

Ryan's exceptional courage is noted not only in the International Brigade hagiographies but also by historians such as James Hopkins who numbered Ryan among four battalion officers who 'earned legendary reputations for their courage and leadership'.[24] Having spent much of his life praising the virtues of militarism, it was just as well Ryan proved so valiant in battle.

For the time being, Ryan's war was over. He was sent to an Alicante hospital to recover and later to Ireland, where he arrived, sun-tanned, arm in sling, in late March 1937. Supposedly home to convalesce, he threw himself into the pro-Republican campaign, speaking at meetings and editing and printing the *Irish Democrat*, the new left-wing newspaper. Ryan's speeches, as Jacob noted, continued to dwell on similarities between Spain and Ireland:

He dwelt mainly on the likenesses of events & parties here & in Spain, sketched the co-operation of Church & O'Duffy Fascists here in 1931 when the pastoral came out against Saor Éire 'in effect an election manifesto for the Cosgrave Govt.' – & how [Ernest] Blythe & [Richard] Mulcahy tried to raise a mutiny in the army, between the election & opening of new Dáil in '32, but the rank & file wdn't back them. If they had succeeded – wdn't [Bishop] Cohalan & [Bishop] Doherty come out & support them 'they'd be out first and the others wdn't be long at their heels'. And the big bankers, landlords, & remnants of the Garrison wd all be with them, and on other side the plain people. Except for having no IRA, the situation in Spain last year was just what Ireld's wd have been if M. & B. had succeeded . . . Spanish workers are winning because all sorts of TUs, & political parties unite in one movement. Ireland must face the Fascist fight now.[25]

But Ireland was not Spain, there was no fascist threat and the 'plain people' remained apathetic or more often hostile to the Spanish Republic (as was illustrated by Ryan's dismal performance in the local elections in the summer of 1937). As with many revolutionaries, Ryan's outlook veered between optimism and delusion. For example, he and O'Donnell believed it possible to build a real 'united front' in Ireland that summer but 'nothing came of the idea. No one seems to remember now what happened'.[26] A more encouraging development was the rapprochement between Congress and the IRA. In the summer of 1937 Ryan printed and even helped to edit *An Phoblacht*, while he and Tom Barry, the new IRA chief of staff, marched together into a hail of police batons at the head of an anti-coronation march. But this co-operation reflected the weakness of both movements; the IRA was in disarray and its leadership divided. Neither *An Phoblacht* nor the *Irish Democrat* survived the year.

By late summer Ryan's thoughts were returning to Spain. He had intended to return when he recuperated, but delayed the journey in order to spend time with his sister Catherine who was dying of tuberculosis. Publicly, Ryan continued to assert that Irishmen should fight in Spain and responded to republican criticism with internationalist rhetoric. He denied they were 'deserting the fight at home' or that they were 'idealists, who come to fight another nation's battles': 'We are here because we are realists . . . if Fascism triumphed in Spain, it would be the beginning of the end for human liberty and progress.'[27] He argued that they went to Spain not just to counter O'Duffy but to 'restore a historical connection with the international struggle that existed in the time of the United Irishmen'.[28] But, as so often with Ryan, there was some distance between his public and private positions. Privately, Ryan played down his internationalism and was ambivalent about returning to Spain. He continued to support the Spanish Republic,

but political circumstances had changed greatly and the motives
behind his original intervention no longer existed. The Christian
Front had collapsed, and, crucially, the Irish Brigade, had returned
home that summer. A private letter, written shortly before his
return to Spain, offers a more accurate insight into his thinking:

> I've no reputation to boast – or to seek – as an internationalist; I came
> home three months ago, more a nationalist than ever . . . I wanted to
> bring out a few hundred men; I could get them; I could bring them. I
> didn't, for I wanted them at home all the more. I go alone, and I'll try
> to save the lives of the few that are left. That's my new role . . . Spain is
> of minor news value in Ireland now . . . Whatever was to be gained on
> the Spanish issue was ours.

Ryan was pessimistic about the Republic's chances of success:
'The liberty of Spain is apparently the price to be paid for staving
off a great war.'[29] Tom Barry recalled: 'I told him that now it is
obvious that Franco had won, he should not return at all. He
reminded me that he had got the survivors out there and his duty
was to help in getting them back to Ireland . . . It was the only
decision an honourable man could take and Frank was certainly
that.' Seán O'Casey had no better luck when he met Ryan in
London – he 'couldn't think of leaving the boys by themselves'.[30]
Ryan confirmed this from jail some years later:

> I came back to Spain just when the return of O'Duffy was
> foreshadowed . . . I considered my mission in Spain ended when he
> was leaving Spain; I came back to pull out men, and so to save lives.
> The number of men who returned to Ireland June to October 1937 is
> evidence. After October the Irish unit existed only in name.[31]

Ryan went back out of a sense of duty more than anything else. It
was a fateful decision and not taken lightly. Nora Harkin, who

attended a farewell party for Ryan at Bobby Edwards's flat, recalled seeing him, sitting out of sight on a step outside the main room, as one of his friends sang a ballad: 'A light was shining on his cheeks – full of tears. He didn't know anyone saw him. I nearly knew what was going through his mind.'[32]

Ryan arrived in Spain in mid-June. His task, as he acknowledged to O'Reilly, his close friend in America, would not be easy: 'Frankly, Gerald, I'm not at all sure of the outcome . . . While I'll try to be back [in Ireland] soon, I'm thinking I'll have to see the job through.'[33] He was successful in securing repatriations for Irishmen between June and September, by which time the great majority of Irishmen had returned (although a small number of CPI members continued to travel to Spain). This suggests that despite his non-communist status and difficulties with Marty and others, Ryan exercised a good deal of influence within the International Brigade command. He was, after all, an extremely useful figure to the brigade authorities: he held the loyalty of the Irish volunteers, he was a skilled propagandist with American connections, and as a prominent non-communist he was an ideal representative of the non-partisan Popular Front image of the brigades.[34] His self-confidence may also have helped; asked about the impact of the Marty dispute, one Irish volunteer observed: 'Frank Ryan wasn't intimidated by him. Frank Ryan wasn't intimidated by anyone.'[35]

But how did Ryan feel about the communists who were increasingly tightening their grip over the Republican army and government? As a brigade staff officer, Ryan, in contrast to most Irish volunteers, was aware of the internal dissensions within Republican Spain: he told Tom Barry of the 'splits, indiscipline, agitators, treachery, groups out for power for themselves and so on among the Spanish Republicans'.[36] Publicly, at least, he supported communist authority in Spain; as a brigade officer and propagandist, he could not have functioned there otherwise. The latter role, in particular, could entail gross distortions of the truth; Ryan, for example, backed the communist denunciation of the anti-Stalinist POUM (Partido Obrero Unificación Marxista) as 'a fascist force in the rear'.[37] He must also have been aware of the brigade command's harsh treatment of its own soldiers which took its cue from the ongoing Stalinist purges in the USSR. For example, recent research from the communist archives in Moscow has revealed that over a quarter of the 2,000 British battalion volunteers were identified as deserters, spies, drunks, cowards, Trotskyites or fascists by the paranoid brigade command and its networks of secret police and informers. Volunteers who clashed with the communists were secretly imprisoned, and in some cases (including at least one Irishman) executed.[38]

Frustratingly, the Communist Party's view of Ryan remains unknown. Despite the fact that the Moscow files on rank-and-file Irish figures extend up to 20 pages each, the file on the most important Irishman in Spain contains only his International Red Help contribution card.[39] Like many in the brigades who were uneasy about communist methods but believed in the Republic's cause, he may have felt that centralised authority was more pragmatic than a divided Republic. Eugene Downing, an Irish volunteer and former CPI member, believed that Ryan felt the Communist Party 'was too disciplined and it dictated to you all the time'.[40] Ryan's anti-authoritarianism was evident in his clashes with Marty and other communists. As with the IRA, he appears to have pragmatically balanced his propagandist work (and the subservience to the communist line which this entailed) with a more sceptical private position. But it must have been a difficult balancing act, and subsequent remarks indicated his suspicion of Soviet influence.

Ryan divided his time in Spain between propaganda work and supporting the Irish volunteers in action. The latter role provided him with material for his radio broadcasts from Madrid and articles for the international left-wing press. In 1937 he began editing the *Book of the XV Brigade*, described by James Hopkins as 'a masterpiece' of Communist Party literature. The British and American commissars gave Ryan the names of volunteers, divided into three categories according to how much prominence each should receive. A good deal of importance was attached to the propaganda value of the book, particularly in Britain and the United States. Naturally, it closely followed the Communist Party's interpretation of events – although when Ryan was reprimanded in March 1938 for not following 'the correct IB line', he privately complained that it was not his fault that 'the line' had changed since Christmas.[41] Whatever his private feelings, Ryan was an important part of the tightly controlled propaganda section of the International Brigades. He was continually moved around and, as a (recently appointed) major on the brigade staff, enjoyed a good deal of latitude and prestige, mixing with such figures as the commander of Madrid, General Miaja, and enjoying some 'wild nights' in Madrid with Ernest Hemingway.[42]

In early 1938, as Ryan was completing the *Book of the XV Brigade* and marking time before his return to Ireland, Franco began an intensive assault to recapture Teruel, recently taken by Republican forces. He was successful on 21 February, around the time Ryan sent his completed book to the printers in Madrid. Yet Ryan lingered on, continually postponing his return. As in the summer of 1937, his loyalty to his remaining men, combined with his pride and courage, kept him in danger long after he had sent home most of those he brought over. Ryan later explained:

> Why did I remain in Spain? . . . When I was getting men home, I was getting the responsibility for their lives off my shoulders, and becoming more of a free agent i.e. more of an individual than a representative. Then pride kept me here; after the fall of Asturias and then

after Teruel I couldn't pull out and be considered 'a rat who left the sinking ship'.[43]

On 9 March, as Ryan prepared to go home, the Nationalists broke through the Aragon front. The Republicans had been unprepared for the advance, and town after town fell. Retreat turned into a rout, and the 15th Brigade, reduced to 500 demoralised and exhausted men, regrouped near the Ebro for a last stand on 15 March. Every available reinforcement, including Ryan, was rushed there to shore up the disintegrating front. Ryan was assigned to the British battalion, which received orders on 30 March to occupy a line of defence at Calaceite, eight miles west of Gandesa. One of the Irish volunteers recalled:

My last meeting with Frank Ryan was the day we were going into one of our last actions in Spain. Frank who was now a Major and wearing full uniform, paid a visit to the British Batt. Some of us didn't recognise him at first as he walked around talking to the lads here and there. He seldom if ever wore any set of military stripes or bars . . . Before leaving for the front a number of the lads which included Jim Regan of Cork known as 'the farmer' and myself went on a deputation to Frank to appeal to him to stay back, as he had been advised to do so by the doctors . . . It was of no use, his final reply was, 'wherever the lads are I will be with them'.[44]

The British battalion set out for Calaceite that night. The following dawn, as they were approaching Calaceite, the lead company, which included Ryan, stumbled on a unit of Italian tanks. Mistaking them for Republican forces, the company marched into their midst and carnage ensued. Around 150 men were killed and another 140 captured. The disaster must be attributed to the fluidity of the lines and the battalion's combination of exhausted and inexperienced soldiers. Extraordinarily, there had been no advance guard to scout the territory. Ryan, as the most senior officer in the battalion, was technically at fault, but he was merely attached to the battalion, not a command officer. Positioned near the head of the advance company, Ryan stood no chance of escape and was captured. His military involvement, if not his struggle against Franco, was at an end.

CHAPTER 4

Collaborator, 1938–44

Notwithstanding the disaster at Calaceite, Ryan met with some luck on the morning of 31 March. International Brigade officers were routinely executed by the Nationalists, but the Italians were more appreciative of the exchange value of foreign prisoners. The lack of details in Ryan's military book also allowed him to claim that he had just arrived at the front, 'so I couldn't know the names of Commands, morale of troops &c. – all of which questions were asked me, with a rifle pointing at my chest, the day of my capture'.[1] Ryan did not disguise his rank and, from the outset, proved an inspiring example to the other prisoners. As they were led away from the front, Ryan demanded food for his men and urged them to remember why they were in Spain. He was separated from the other captives and brought to Zaragoza for execution, but his presence was discovered by a foreign journalist, who publicised the fact that he had been captured alive.[2] Ryan rejoined the other prisoners in San Pedro de Cardena in early April.

San Pedro, a monastery on the outskirts of Burgos, held 700 foreign prisoners in poor conditions. They were beaten if they refused to sing the Nationalist anthem or salute its flag, as well as for other misdemeanours. With his prison experience, Ryan was aware of the importance of sustaining morale through unity and measured resistance. He refused to give the fascist salute, arguing that a military salute was sufficient. One prisoner recollected that

Ryan often complained about their conditions to the prison commandant and visiting journalists: 'Several times during our first week of capture, he was taken from us and put in the condemned cells where he thought, as all of us did, that he was going to be shot.'[3] Ryan was soon transferred from San Pedro, and the other prisoners again assumed he had been executed. His special treatment reflected not only his rank but also his troublesome behaviour. The *New York Times* journalist, William Carney, who was hostile to the Republican cause, told the Irish minister to Spain, Leopold Kerney, that after Ryan's removal 'the American prisoners in San Pedro de Cardena have become much more docile'.[4]

Ryan had been brought from San Pedro to face a court martial – in this period a formality before execution. He received the death sentence on 15 June after the standard kangaroo trial. Ryan's only contact with a defence counsel had been 'a few moments' conversation' on the morning of the trial. The main evidence against him was an anonymous letter detailing various murders he was purported to have committed in Ireland, including those of Kevin O'Higgins and Vice-Admiral Somerville. Franco's Irish supporters were behind much of the 'evidence' – Eoin O'Duffy's subordinate in Spain, Tom Gunning, was overheard complaining: 'For two months I have been trying to get them to shoot him, and they won't shoot him.'[5] Ryan's attitude was stoical: 'At my trial I wasn't interested much in my life, believing it already forfeit. I took up the attitude that I was a prisoner of war, if they wanted to shoot prisoners of war OK, but I objected to being shot on the evidence of an anonymous letter.'[6] But there was some strategy behind Ryan's defence: 'He explained that his chief reason for going to Spain was that O'Duffy was misrepresenting Ireland, describing him more or less as a British agent.'[7] (Throughout the next two years Ryan emphasised his anti-Britishness rather than pro-Republicanism, even telling the pro-Nationalist Duchess of

Tetuan that 'he had made a mistake in going to Spain, but that he could not make any confession of that kind before a Tribunal'.[8] Ryan also stood up for himself: 'In the end I told them I didn't want any clemency or mercy – as the Defender had asked – that I had observed the rules of war, such as they are; that I'd done nothing of which I was ashamed, and that I was a soldier in the army of a Govt. which the Govt. of my country recognised.'[9] If nothing else this impressed his captors: 'As he left the court, he was saluted respectfully by civil guards and others present.'[10] But it was probably also astute. A Nationalist official reported 'that there is a certain respect, if not for Ryan's attitude, for his truthfulness and bravery'.[11] Nonetheless, he was sentenced to death on the basis that he had been an 'outstanding figure' of the Irish republican movement, had fought in the International Brigades, and – more damagingly – had campaigned against Franco in Ireland and voluntarily returned to the 'Red Army'. The judge's rather Orwellian finding was that Ryan was guilty of rebellion 'against the Legitimate Government of the Nation which the Army united on 18th July 1936'.[12]

However, the sentence was not immediately carried out, and a number of influential figures worked to save his life. Captain Meade, a Spanish Nationalist who served in the Irish Brigade, worked with Kerney to undermine the case against Ryan. His case also received support from abroad: de Valera, the Irish papal nuncio and the British Foreign Office pleaded for clemency. By the following month he was out of immediate danger, although an official told Kerney that 'there had been a critical moment when it was just touch and go whether he would be "popped off"'.[13]

After his trial Ryan was transferred to Burgos Central Prison, where he spent the next two years. In the meantime a well-organised campaign to secure Ryan's freedom began. Demonstrations were held in Dublin, Belfast, London and throughout the United States.

Numerous organisations passed resolutions calling for his release and the less than convincing slogan 'Release Frank Ryan or else' began to appear on walls throughout Ireland. Over 50 Dáil deputies and senators signed a petition, while even Eoin O'Duffy appealed to Franco for clemency. In Britain over 70 members of the House of Commons signed a petition, while in the United States Gerald O'Reilly claimed that 'Practically every large American city has an active Frank Ryan Release Committee.'[14] Ryan had become perhaps the most famous political prisoner of the Spanish Civil War, but, as Kerney pointed out, the effectiveness of the campaign was questionable: 'Spain is not a democratic country; public opinion does not count; a tearing, raging mass campaign in other countries would be simply laughed at by the authorities here, & those who may think otherwise know nothing of present-day Spain.'[15] Kerney was also disappointed by the attitude of the Republican government which refused to exchange a high-ranking Italian officer for Ryan.[16]

But there were also less public forces working against Ryan. Although the British representative in Burgos, Sir Robert Hodgson, had told Kerney and his own government that he was working on Ryan's behalf, Captain Meade informed Kerney that Hodgson had denounced Ryan as a 'gangster' in Nationalist circles.[17] His duplicity was confirmed when Carney of the *New York Times* told Kerney that 'Hodgson had done his best to see that Ryan was kept in prison, and that he (Hodgson) was a close relative of Somerville, who had been assassinated in Ireland'.[18] Kerney also learned that 'Franco had received a great many letters from Ireland saying that Ryan was a dangerous man and begging Franco not to release him'.[19] Ryan blamed the Jesuits (who were also plaguing him in Burgos) for this, while Kerney named Bishop Fogarty of Killaloe.[20] By late 1939 Kerney was becoming desperate. Although almost all foreign prisoners had been released, there was no sign of progress on

Ryan's case. The Kafkaesque nature of Nationalist bureaucracy proved demoralising: 'The Franco attitude is that their justice is unquestionable, that they are the sole judges and that they on no account render to anyone for what they do in Spain; as far as I know, even the British Agent in Burgos has never been able to ascertain what crimes are imputed to Frank Ryan.'[21] In April 1940 Kerney reported: 'I am struck now and again by some stray remarks in the course of conversations that there is secret opposition from another country than Ireland.'[22] When Dublin rejected Kerney's suggestion of getting Ryan out of jail by means of a trade agreement, Kerney resolved on an extreme course which would have fateful implications.

Ryan served his time with characteristic stoicism. In late 1939 Kerney reported: 'Ryan showed no signs at all of impatience and he accepts his position philosophically, although he confessed that it cast a shadow over him now and again when he reflected on the fact that as time passed his parents were becoming more aged but he was not worrying about himself.'[23] In November 1939 Ryan was relieved to learn that his death sentence had been commuted to 30 years, as unreprieved prisoners in Burgos were being shot, with four hours' notice, at the rate of 20 a week. He was reportedly the only remaining officer not to have been executed.[24] Conditions were poor owing to overcrowding, hunger and disease. Five times the usual number of prisoners had been incarcerated, and it was difficult to find space in the dormitories to lie down at night.[25] Weather permitting, the prisoners spent the day ambling around the prison square. Food was in short supply; Ryan's daily ration consisted of one cup of malt coffee, one small loaf of bread and four small cups of watery soup. This was supplemented with private parcels and frequent trips to the hospital, where meat and eggs were available, but Ryan's weight dropped from 13½ stone to 12 stone, and he was increasingly troubled by rheumatism and heart problems. But prisoners were allowed to congregate, and Ryan, as Kerney reported, was reasonably well placed among the hierarchy of prisoners: 'Ryan has managed to cultivate friendly relations with more or less influential prisoners, and there are ways and means of making fairly satisfactory arrangements under such conditions.'[26]

Ryan spent much of his time teaching English. Kerney and Father Mulrean, the eccentric former chaplain of General O'Duffy's Irish Brigade, often visited him. Ryan was grateful for Mulrean's services, as the compulsory prison mass, celebrated by an obnoxious armed chaplain, took place underneath a portrait of Franco and concluded with a fascist salute.[27] These visits, and the volume of mail posted to Ryan from around the world, ensured that the warders treated him well. The chief warder told Kerney: 'They respected him in the prison, and he had never been punished, although he had at times intervened between subordinate warders and prisoners whom they were maltreating – much to the astonishment of the warders.'[28] Ryan did not passively submit to the prison regime. A Nationalist diplomat told Kerney he was 'still being troublesome and expresses his condition as "alive and kicking"'.[29]

Beyond Burgos, the Nazi–Soviet Non-Aggression Pact and the outbreak of the Second World War were rapidly transforming the political landscape. His closest friend in prison, Tom Jones, subsequently recalled that Ryan's 'ideals had developed towards socialism and his association with the British Battalion had undoubtedly given him a different view of English working people. He was extremely angry when the IRA started their campaign of bombings in England in 1939. He classified them as irresponsible lunatics who were doing the maximum damage to the Irish Republic [*sic*] and to the future unity of the whole of Ireland.' Jones claimed that Ryan even requested him to pass on the names of several people he blamed for the campaign to the British

embassy: 'Frank believed that the whole of Ireland would eventually re-unite, not so much by force of arms but through British
and world public opinion and by agreement with the Protestant
people of Northern Ireland.' News of the Non-Aggression Pact
also troubled him: 'Frank became very upset and talked about it for
days. He was strongly of the opinion that Russia was going Fascist
and that this was the reason for the deal.' Like Kerney, Ryan
became increasingly frustrated by his continued incarceration.
When Jones was released, Ryan instructed him to inform the IRA
'that if he was not released from prison and allowed to leave Spain
within 6 months . . . the IRA should blow up every Spanish Embassy
in the western world'.[30]

Leopold Kerney was embarking on a similarly dramatic course
of events. In late 1939 he employed a Spanish lawyer, Baron Jaime
de Champourcin, with dubious connections (or, as he put it,
'certain friendships about which I find it discreet not to enquire').[31]
Kerney had learnt that Franco had instructed that Ryan should
never be released without his personal permission, and de
Champourcin, who had contacts within both German and Spanish
military intelligence, represented his last throw of the dice.
Kerney claimed that de Champourcin suggested to him that 'the
Gestapo might serve to secure Ryan's liberation'. Kerney agreed,
although it was actually Abwehr (German military intelligence)
rather than the Gestapo whose Madrid officials were promptly
instructed by Berlin to secure Ryan's freedom. Franco refused to
release Ryan, presumably to avoid diplomatic complications, but
agreed to permit an 'escape'. At 2 a.m. on 25 July Ryan was taken
from prison and handed over to Abwehr on the French border.
Kerney's report of this remarkable event led to turmoil within the
Department of External Affairs. The potential implications for
Irish neutrality of a diplomat facilitating the transfer of Ireland's
highest-profile political prisoner to Nazi Germany were serious.

Moreover, as Kerney acknowledged, Franco had ordered this 'very unusual procedure, as a concession to Germany', not Ireland.[32] Kerney's role in this episode has remained contested and mysterious. It has been claimed that de Valera approved Ryan's release, but – at a time when the Irish government was executing republicans due to the danger of IRA collaboration with Germany – this seems unlikely.[33] Moreover, Kerney later told G2 (Irish military intelligence) that he 'had no means of getting a decision on that matter from the Dept of External Affairs so he took upon himself the responsibility' of agreeing to Ryan's release.[34]

But Kerney was only part of the equation; two old friends of Ryan, Elizabeth Clissmann (*née* Mulcahy) and her husband, Helmut, were also central. Clissmann was an officer in the section of Abwehr which dealt with foreign revolutionary movements of potential use to Germany. When the Clissmanns learnt of Ryan's incarceration, they brought his case to the attention of Abwehr, pointing out that, as an anti-English republican, he could counter Allied propaganda in the United States.[35] Kerney, Clissmann and Ryan all insisted that each of these efforts to secure his freedom was made independently of the other, but when other evidence is considered, this seems unlikely. Certain aspects of Kerney's story remain suspicious. Kerney denied knowing Ryan before his incarceration, but Elizabeth Clissmann had invited both men to her Dublin flat in 1937 where, she recalled, they had got on well. Clissmann had also been a close friend of Kerney since before her marriage, and had lived in his Paris apartment for almost a year.[36] Given that both were attempting to secure Ryan's liberty for a lengthy period, were in touch with each other, and that the successful attempt involved co-operation between Abwehr and Kerney (with de Champourcin as the link), it seems implausible that there was not some degree of co-operation. Kerney's initiative may have been humane but was clearly unprofessional. A committed republican rather than a

career civil servant, his actions may have been politically motivated. After interviewing Kerney, G2 reported: 'The Minister
formed a very favourable opinion of Ryan, he was an idealist and
a man of very high principles . . . The Minister had no doubt
that Frank Ryan went willingly to Germany and was apparently
anxious to collaborate with the Germans on some basis . . . He
did not believe that Ryan would do anything underhand but would
be inspired by his desire for the return of the Six Counties as part
of the national territory.'[37]

Ryan's motives are less difficult to understand. He faced two
options in July 1940 – to remain in jail indefinitely, or accept
Abwehr's help in securing his release. Ryan believed that Abwehr
would either allow him to return to Ireland or, as Clissmann had
suggested, to the United States to mobilise Irish–American opinion
against Britain. His deteriorating health must have influenced his
decision; by 1940 he was almost totally deaf and was described as
'shrunken and worn . . . like an old man'.[38] But, unknown to Ryan,
Abwehr had other plans. In the summer of 1940 it had approved
Operation Dove, a mission to send the IRA's chief of staff, Seán
Russell, to Ireland by submarine, and it was now decided that Ryan
should accompany him. Russell, like most of the IRA leadership,
saw the war as an opportunity to secure an ally against Britain and
had spent several months in Germany studying sabotage techniques.
Abwehr was unsure as to how Ryan, the socialist republican dissi-
dent, and Russell, who typified the apolitical militarist IRA outlook,
would react, but when they met on 4 August they agreed to travel
together. Abwehr recorded that Russell and Ryan were not given a
specific mission, but rather 'the chance to exploit Ireland's hour' in
whatever way they felt suitable. The mission was considered
important: Admiral Dönitz personally assigned an experienced
U-boat commander, Korvettenkapitän von Stockhausen, to the
mission, and his crew was warned that any loose talk would be

punished by death.[39] On 8 August both men left Wilhelmshaven on board the U-65, along with a cargo of radio and demolition equipment. But on 14 August, as the U-boat approached the west coast of Ireland, Russell died from a perforated ulcer. The submarine commander asked Ryan if he wished to continue or return to Germany. Despite claims to the contrary, the declassified documents of the U-65 mission, as well as the evidence of the key figures in Germany, confirm that Ryan freely chose to return to Germany.

It was this decision which marked a crucial shift in Ryan's attitude from an understandable desire merely to use German assistance as a means of securing safe passage home to a conscious determination to act in a way intended to facilitate republican collaboration in some capacity with Nazi Germany. Significantly, a recently released British intelligence report, based on the interrogation of Ryan's German handlers, indicated his willingness to collaborate with the Germans, albeit to advance republican goals. It noted: 'The German motive for sending Ryan was that Russell throughout his stay in Germany had shown considerable reticence towards the Germans and plainly did not regard himself as a German agent ... By sending Ryan, Abw[ehr] II felt that their own interests would be better safeguarded, as Ryan accepted more easily his position as a German agent.'[40]

Why did Ryan, Ireland's most celebrated anti-fascist, agree to such a course of action? Ryan's subsequent explanation, according to Elizabeth Clissmann, was that he did not know the details of Russell's mission, including his radio codes and contacts, and was reluctant to meet a suspicious and disappointed IRA.[41] But if Ryan was merely along for the ride and opposed to the IRA's collaboration with Nazi Germany – as his many defenders subsequently claimed – his ignorance of Russell's mission was surely irrelevant. The real question is: why, by returning to Germany, did Ryan choose to facilitate some form of republican collaboration with Germany? His motives can, perhaps, be best understood in the context of the international position in the summer of 1940. Germany had effortlessly overrun much of western Europe in a few short months. Italy had recently joined on Germany's side, while the United States and the Soviet Union had remained neutral. It appeared inevitable that Germany would now invade Britain, or that Britain would invade Ireland in anticipation of a German invasion (Ryan tended to the latter view). Either way, the status of Northern Ireland was up for grabs. Kerney suggested that Ryan placed this opportunity over other factors, a view broadly confirmed by Elizabeth Clissmann, who maintains that Ryan was under no illusions about the trustworthiness of the Nazi regime but wished to be in a position to influence the decision which would have to be made about partition.[42]

Ryan, for his part, had previously stated that the next world war would provide 'Ireland's opportunity'. In 1931 he wrote: 'England will be engaged in another great war soon. Then she will try to take advantage of the provisions of the Treaty for garrisoning ports in Ireland. That will be the end of England's rule in Ireland.'[43] The ports had been returned, but there is little reason to think Ryan had significantly changed his views. Ryan would not have viewed his decision as 'collaboration' with the moral connotations the term now carries. Although it may seem shocking, Ryan – like many Irish republicans – did not believe the Second World War pitted a morally superior side against a morally inferior one. Aside from the influence of the Nazi-Soviet Non-Aggression Pact, which ensured that many on the radical left initially viewed the war as an amoral struggle between rival imperialist powers, Ryan felt Britain was no better than Germany. Irish republicans – and not only extremists – had an enormous capacity for self-delusion when it came to the question of the relative nature of British oppression. For Ryan, the real issue was that the *realpolitik* of 1940 – as in 1916 – indicated that republican self-interest lay in co-operation with Germany. As on previous occasions when Ryan's progressive values conflicted with his traditional republican aspirations, the latter prevailed.

Following Russell's death, Ryan returned to Berlin, where he became an adviser on Irish affairs. It has been argued that Ryan's presence in Germany was not as anomalous as might seem, since, under the leadership of Admiral Canaris, Abwehr was one of the few pockets of anti-Nazi sentiment. But for most of Ryan's time in Germany, all Irish operations – Abwehr and Foreign Office – were directed by a special department run by Dr Edmund Veesenmayer, an SS officer on secondment to the Foreign Office. Veesenmayer was a committed Nazi, a powerful and intimidating figure with access to senior ministers and something of a trouble-shooter, overseeing such sensitive tasks as the orchestration of foreign coups and the extermination of half a million Jews as Gauleiter of Hungary. But, judging from a letter smuggled to Kerney in December 1940, Ryan seemed reasonably content under Veesenmayer. Abwehr had assured him that he had been unconditionally freed under its protection: 'Thanks to all that', he wrote, 'I enjoy the status of a "gentleman at large". Looking on at a war is rather a novel experience for me, and – for a change – not a disagreeable one.' His only complaint was that he had not been able to go home or to the United States. Ryan was at pains to assure Kerney that he would not act against Irish interests: 'If you have any qualms of conscience about possible bad results of your intervention on my behalf – then, Don't. I remain my own master . . . nobody can make me do anything I don't want to do. Incidentally, no one has ever tried here – a thing which surprised me at first, but no longer does. I have met only gentlemen.'[44]

That Ryan did not feel compromised is not as strange as it sounds, given German support for Irish neutrality. As he explained to Kerney in late 1941,

There is a very definite hands-off policy with regard to the little
island. The Foreign Office chokes off everybody who tries to interfere
there . . . The office is apparently dominated by the fear that Sam [the
United States] or John [Britain] would find an excuse to step in there . . .
The office appears very satisfied by your Boss' [de Valera's] unyield-
ing attitude towards Sam & John. They look upon him as a future
potential friend.[45]

The Foreign Office viewed neutrality, with its denial of valuable
ports to Britain, as the next best thing to Irish support for
Germany – an option which remained unrealistic in the absence
of a successful German invasion of Britain. For this reason Ryan
was not placed under pressure but rather 'treated – not merely officially but genuinely – as a "distinguished guest" . . . My status –
that of a non-party neutral – is established. I act merely in a
"consultative" capacity – my views are asked when there are
situations and news that require interpretations.' Interestingly,
Ryan also claimed he was not a representative of the IRA: 'I am
not working for any organisation at home. (I do not even know if
such organisation is aware of my whereabouts.)'[46] This was possible, as the Germans had become increasingly disillusioned with
the IRA's incompetence.

But despite the confident tone of his letters Ryan was playing a
risky game. His decision to go to Germany was based on the likelihood of either a German invasion of Britain or a British invasion
of Ireland. De Valera's policy in the latter eventuality was clear. If
Britain invaded Ireland, his government would accept German
help to defend itself. In this scenario, Ryan would be a well-placed
and influential figure, co-ordinating German support for Ireland
as Roger Casement had done in the First World War, rallying
extreme republicans behind de Valera, and invading Northern
Ireland. But if Germany invaded Ireland, de Valera would accept

British help, leaving Ryan in an impossible position. Ryan had considered both scenarios. In late 1940 he informed Kerney: 'Nothing bad has resulted from the affair [his escape], and now, with the changed situation at home – nothing bad can.' The 'changed situation' probably refers to Germany's failure to win the air superiority over the Channel necessary for an invasion.[47] Ryan seems to be hinting at both invasion scenarios in his letter to Kerney in late 1941:

> There might be a situation in which I might go as a liaison to your Boss!!! There might also be a situation (I was always a pessimist) in which I might be asked to do something I don't like . . . If the unlikely should ever happen, sit yez down aisy! For – I won't do the dirty. And when you plan my tombstone let it be of granite – like my stubborn cranium contents . . . And, again, there might be a continuation of the situation in which I find myself – the guest of a sentimental family, and drawing double rations, and having too much leisure.[48]

It was the final outcome which ultimately prevailed. Following Germany's attack on the Soviet Union in June 1941, an invasion of Britain was no longer likely. Ryan had miscalculated and became increasingly disillusioned as the war dragged on. Veesenmayer's department continued to formulate ambitious plans involving Ryan: in late 1940, for example, Operation Whale proposed to fly Ryan secretly to Ireland to act as a military liaison with Germany in the eventuality of an allied invasion. Veesenmayer valued Ryan not only as an IRA contact but as an influential republican who could be useful in 'bringing about an understanding between the IRA and de Valera' and 'in the event of Ireland's occupation by England or America, to organise the resistance'. Veesenmayer, perhaps knowingly, exaggerated the influence of Ryan, who did not exactly have the claimed 'extensive connections with . . . de Valera himself, as well as to the Irish regular army, the nationalist Irishmen in Northern Ireland, and especially to leading Irishmen in America'.[49] By the summer of 1941 Abwehr's plan had expanded into Operation Sea Eagle:

> The Reich Minister for Foreign Affairs [Joachim von Ribbentrop] intends to propose to the Führer that the former contact man of Abwehr II, Frank Ryan should go to Ireland . . . in order to incite the IRA and generally the Irish people to resistance against a possibly planned occupation by America or England.[50]

Of course, whether Ryan would have acted as Veesenmayer intended or simply wanted to return home can not be known. It is also unlikely that he could have successfully carried out such a mission, given the IRA's disarray and the strong public support for neutrality within southern Ireland. However, owing to the increasing importance of the Eastern Front, Hitler postponed Sea Eagle, and Ryan rarely featured in German military plans subsequently. But he continued to hold a high opinion of Veesenmayer ('He has been most persistent and successful in preventing dealings with certain people in the little island. His attitude on all questions is that of his Chief; hence his insistence that the status quo in the little island is not to be interfered with is significant') and continued to hope that Germany might be drawn into a liberating invasion of Ireland.[51] In early 1942 he told Kerney: 'I had the feeling, last December, that Mr Sam would tell Mr Bull that now is the right time (seeing Mr Jerry is occupied elsewhere) – to grab the Irish ports . . . They might try it now – Sam taking the leading part. And, of course, we'd have to have help in driving them out. And, the immediate result would be the occupation of at least our ports for 5 (or 50?!) years – by one or other side, – until they have finished their war'. Despite his protestations of neutrality, Ryan felt that even a German victory 'wouldn't be so bad as what would happen us if ultimately Sam & Bull were to win' – an outcome many Irish republicans but few of his left-wing friends desired. Failing an invasion, Ryan hoped 'we may be left in peace until the Bull is weak enough for us to get our own'.[52] This letter, like much of the evidence concerning Ryan's time in Germany, suggests an extraordinary naïvety about the likely outcome of German occupation which is difficult to reconcile with his anti-fascist background. Hitler was unlikely to favour Ireland over Britain in any post-war settlement – and how could Ryan have failed to consider the implications of German occupation for Irish Jews, communists and other enemies of fascism?

Increasingly Ryan's thoughts turned to home. He told Kerney: 'I want to get back – so that I can play a part (and I really believe I could do a little) in unifying my friends to support Dev in his foreign policy, while reserving our rights to differ in other matters. Here, they raise the objection that my appearance at home, now, would make Bull think I'm coming in with "orders of the day", and that a crisis would be precipitated.'[53] Although Ryan doubted this, the Germans were correct: de Valera insisted that Ryan should not be allowed to return during the war, as it 'would entail all sorts of complications'.[54]

Ryan's life in Germany was a comfortable one, as Veesenmayer's status ensured that he was well treated. In May 1942 he wrote: 'Eating & Sleeping are my main occupation. Otherwise, regard me as one of the unemployed – or more accurately, of the idle rich, both rarities in this country, nowadays. So far as comforts go, I lack nothing. I have special privileges with regard to food and clothes . . . I get everything I ask for except a deportation ticket.'[55] Three months later he noted: 'My position here remains the same. There is no attempt to influence me – unless you can call kindness, hospitality, and frankness attempts.'[56] Yet some discontent was increasingly evident as Germany's fortunes declined. In mid-1942 Ryan told Kerney: 'Time hangs heavily on my hands; that is the only drawback. Partly from the necessity of maintaining an incognito & partly from choice, my range of friends is very small.'[57]

With the exception of Francis Stuart, a republican writer employed as a radio broadcaster by the Nazis, Ryan did not associate with the Irish expatriates in Berlin, an unappealing coterie of fascists and chancers, largely employed in espionage and propaganda. Stuart's recollections are unreliable. He initially claimed to have liked Ryan, but in later years presented a different picture of their relationship. Stuart was struck by the company Ryan kept when they met one evening in 1941: 'In the club, off the Kurfürstendamm, we drank two or three bottles of champagne. We met two of Ryan's friends. One was wearing his party swastika badge on a little gold plaque, which meant he was a founder member of the Nazi Party. I thought it was funny – because these were rare and extremely influential people – that Frank Ryan, who had come from the International Brigade in Spain, had such a friend.'[58] Stuart further recollected:

> Ryan was in a very ambiguous position; starting off fighting for the International Brigade and ending up as an adviser to the SS Colonel Veesenmayer, a Jew exterminator. I never liked Ryan, we didn't really get on . . . I remember one day we were both walking down to the university where I had a class. We disagreed over something. He said to me, 'When' – not 'if', mind you – 'Germany wins the war I will be a minister in the Irish government.' I took this as some sort of threat to me to keep in with him.[59]

However, Ryan was not the only one in an ambiguous position, and it is difficult to know how much credibility to attach to the reminiscences of Stuart, who spent his post-war life reimagining

his collaborationist role in Berlin.[60] But Ryan did have some influence in Germany. When John Codd, an Irish spy, ran into difficulties
in 1942, Ryan secured his release from jail. Codd claimed that
Ryan told him to learn draughts to pass the time and, bizarrely, that
a Russian woman mended his socks. He told Codd also that
'anything he might do to help the Germans would be all right so
far as the Irish organisations in [the] USA are concerned'.[61] He
also visited a prisoner-of-war camp in Friesack to vet Irishmen
for a mooted 'Irish Brigade', but was unenthusiastic about the
proposal.[62] Other sources suggest that Ryan continued to support
Irish neutrality. In 1942 Ryan advised Stuart that his propaganda
broadcasts should contain no anti-Russian bias and defend Irish
neutrality.[63] In 1943 when he was asked for his opinion on a scheme
to incite Irish-American opinion against Roosevelt, Ryan strongly
opposed it on the grounds that it could threaten Irish neutrality.[64]

As the war dragged on, and an invasion of England became
more unlikely, Ryan's usefulness to the Germans declined. Stuart
felt that 'although he was well treated . . . I don't think he'd any
more importance for them'.[65] Ryan's health, which had been poor
since Burgos, began to fail. In early 1943 he suffered a stroke which
left his left side partially paralysed. He recovered that summer, but
spent much of the autumn hospitalised with stomach ulcers. In
January 1944 he recovered sufficiently to agree to meet Dr Hans
Hartmann, the head of the radio service which broadcast propaganda to Ireland, who wanted to employ him. Ryan tried to
maintain some semblance of his 'neutral' status ('If Hartmann can
give me translation work in Luxembourg I've no objection to
giving him my opinion whenever he wants it'), but the distinction
lacks credibility.[66] But the trip to Luxembourg was postponed when
he developed pneumonia and heart problems in February 1944.
Elizabeth Clissmann, worried about his loneliness, 'very depressed'
state and unlikelihood of recovery, asked Kerney if he could be

repatriated.[67] De Valera refused. He was unconvinced by the reports of Ryan's ill-health and dismissed his request for repatriation as 'quite out of the question' for security reasons.[68] Veesenmayer offered to send him to Switzerland, but Ryan declined; at least in Germany he had access to medical care and rations. Towards the end Ryan presented a tragic figure. Francis Stuart recalled:

> Poor Frank died very miserably . . . He was extremely deaf and wouldn't hear the raid warnings. He was extremely ill too, and very homesick in the end. I had great sympathy for him. It was not a question of whether I got on with him or didn't. He had a very miserable end, virtually kept as a prisoner in a sanatorium . . . He was completely disillusioned with them [the Germans] in the end.[69]

Ryan recovered sufficiently to leave his Dresden sanatorium in the early summer of 1944, but in June he developed pleurisy and returned there. On Saturday 10 June, after further heart complications, he slipped into unconsciousness and died. His funeral, attended by Stuart and a small group of friends, was held on 14 June in Loschwitz, near Dresden, where he was buried. A telegram from Berlin adds a curious but potentially significant postscript. The Irish minister in Berlin, asked to verify Ryan's death, reported that 'The Foreign Office promised to send me . . . [the] medical report which indicates basic cause of death was syphilis contracted 1937.'[70] However, the subsequent medical report, which attributed Ryan's death to 'an organic disease of the heart and vascular system of the central nervous system', did not specify syphilis as the cause of death.[71] Moreover, Ryan had suffered from heart problems since the mid-1930s. Was this an attempt by the German authorities to discredit Ryan? If not, the fact that he had been slowly dying from syphilis, a degenerative disease of the body and brain, must have affected Ryan's behaviour in the final years.

Interviewed three decades later – after having served six years of his Nuremberg sentence for his not inconsiderable role in the Holocaust – Veesenmayer maintained that Ryan (whom he disliked) had died of syphilis.[72] Like much else about Frank Ryan's mysterious final years, the truth may never be known.

Conclusion

Almost 60 years after his death Frank Ryan has been the subject of biographies, documentaries, ballads, novels and much academic debate.[1] With the exception of Michael Collins, one historian recently asserted, he 'is now the most admired political figure of modern Ireland'.[2] This seems unlikely, but there is no doubting Ryan's prominence as a 'patron saint of the Irish Republican Left', a status which contrasts with his relative lack of success in his own lifetime.[3] This is all the more surprising given that Ryan, unlike other republican heroes, did not leave behind a body of writing to influence future generations. His elevation to prominence did not occur gradually but as a result of changing perceptions of his legacy and its conscious manipulation by those who have claimed a stake in it since the 1970s.

The international left greeted the news of Ryan's death in Nazi Germany with disbelief. *Reynolds News*, which had reported among other rumours that Ryan was fighting with Tito's partisans, suspected he was murdered by Spanish fascists.[4] *Irish Freedom* refused to believe that Ryan willingly stayed in Berlin, while the *Canadian Tribune* compared his comfortable clinic with 'those German sanatoriums in Majdanek and other places'.[5] Ryan's Irish friends were no less bemused. A commemoration committee was formed, but it was evident from its first meeting that there was much concern about Ryan's presence in Germany. Peadar O'Donnell declared that

'Frank Ryan had become a symbol and would come to mean a great deal more in the Republican movement' but alluded to the war years only by noting lamely that Ryan had 'lived in retirement in Germany' devoting himself to 'Irish questions'. Hanna Sheehy Skeffington declared: 'There was no apology required for anything Frank Ryan did or did not do',[6] a remark that appeared to suggest otherwise. The committee commissioned a short biography, but, anticipating further revelations of collaboration, decided not to publish it.[7]

In the long term Ryan's presence in Germany did not prove as damaging as feared. Reliable information was slow to come to light, and, as in the case of that other, more complicit, collaborator, Francis Stuart, few people seemed inclined to examine his actual involvement with the Nazi regime too deeply. Seán Cronin's biography exonerated Ryan from the charge of collaboration: 'He worked for no one. He was his own master. His views were those of an Irish Republican and when asked he gave them.'[8] Cronin accepted Ryan's description of himself as a 'non–party neutral' working only to support Irish neutrality and resist a British invasion. There was much truth in this, but it glossed over uncomfortable issues – not least the fundamentally compromising fact that Ryan was in Berlin offering his advice to Nazi Germany. Cronin's interpretation has been widely accepted, particularly among left-wing and republican historians, who view Ryan more as a victim of the war than of his own miscalculations. One recent account described him as 'a pawn in the political game', while another unconvincingly attributed his decision to return to Germany to his inability 'to break the news of Russell's death to old comrades'.[9] Several other accounts misleadingly claim that Ryan was forced to return to Germany following Russell's death, and that he remained there as a prisoner or 'involuntary guest'.[10] Had Ryan lived it would have proved more difficult to overlook the inconsistencies of his actions during the Second World War.

In the 1970s, by which time the popular perception of the Spanish Civil War had shifted from that of a communist war against Catholicism to a conflict between progressive democratic values and fascism, Ryan's stock began to rise. As the leader of the Irish in Spain, Ryan personified this more idealistic interpretation, and a certain tragic glamour was attached to his early death. Because Ryan could not be identified with a specific political ideology, his legacy was his dramatic life and thus something of a blank canvas. The fact that Ryan had often espoused anti-democratic values throughout his revolutionary career in inter-war Ireland was overlooked as he was transformed into a progressive symbol of anti-fascism, a legacy which served to link the moral victors of the Spanish Civil War with those who daubed '*No pasarán*' on the walls of the Garvaghy road. The endurance of the uncomplicated heroic image of Ryan may also lie in the willingness of Irish people to ignore the more complex reality of Irish (and particularly Irish republican) responses to the Spanish Civil War and Second World War. (Other figures less amenable to rehabilitation, such as Seán Russell, have been less feted by the republican tradition.)[11]

Irish politics had also changed in other respects by the 1970s. Ryan's departure to Spain coincided with the failure of socialist republican ideology. But, following its revival as a central ideology of republicanism during the 'Troubles', Ryan's legacy became more relevant than that of better-known physical-force patriots. Just as commemoration proved useful for Ryan throughout his lifetime, Ryan was commemorated by later republicans, either to glorify the republican tradition or justify a specific political perspective. For example, Peadar O'Donnell's preface to Ryan's biography (itself written by a former IRA chief of staff) advocated a conception of republicanism at variance with the Provisional IRA: 'What must not be lost sight of by those who would invoke Ryan's name to sanction and inspire their activities is that he saw the role of the

IRA as the highest point of intelligence and courage in the youth of a mass movement.'[12]

The Irish communist movement also used Ryan's legacy to promote its own agenda. The process began while he was still alive. In 1936 communist propaganda depicted the International Brigades as a symbol of the united front of socialists and democrats against fascism, but by 1940, after the Non-Aggression Pact had allied the USSR with Nazi Germany, Ryan had become 'the personification of this country's fight against . . . Imperialist "democracies"'.[13] Ryan, a cynic might observe, had died for the party line rather than for any particular political values. His grave in East Germany became a site of commemoration for Irish communists eager to co-opt Ryan's legacy for Stalinism.

Given the multitude of organisations claiming a stake in Ryan, it was to be expected that his legacy would be fought over, but perhaps not also that his corpse would. A republican-backed attempt by the Irish-German Society to secure his remains from the German Democratic Republic was blocked by Irish communists on the grounds that the former were eager to 'play down his anti-fascist record and to deliver a blow against all progressive forces in our country'.[14] The communists counter-attacked, but were blocked by Eilís Ryan, who told the Irish government she was 'anxious that his remains should not now be used by these people to boost the cause of international communism which he never favoured during his life'.[15] In 1979 it was agreed to reinter Ryan as a 'staunch anti-fascist' in Glasnevin's Republican Plot. Eilís placed his remains under the auspices of the National Graves Association to prevent the CPI and the IRA from claiming his legacy. The Provisional IRA's offer of a guard of honour was declined, and the family asked the communists to allow the burial to remain a family affair.[16]

Ryan's remains arrived in Dublin on 21 June 1979, after an exhumation with full military honours in East Germany. He would have been bemused to find the *Irish Times* describing his return as 'an event of historic importance'. The newspaper was confident that Ryan's republican legacy was 'no narrow sectarian doctrine; but one much removed from the sordid activities that debase so much of Republicanism today'.[17] Despite his family's request for a non-political event, Ryan's burial became something of a free for all. Eilís recalled: 'The Communist Party took control when we got the coffin and marched in front of the television'. The East German minister plenipotentiary drew attention to the absence of diplomatic relations with Ireland, declaring that Ryan would 'always remain an unbreakable link between Ireland and my country'.[18] The funeral was attended by leaders from every shade of republicanism from Fianna Fáil to Sinn Féin The Workers' Party. The following day, Ruairí Ó Brádaigh, the president of Provisional Sinn Féin, delivered an oration at Ryan's grave, at which wreaths were laid by the Provisional IRA Army Council and the Basque paramilitary organisation ETA, among others.[19] Ryan would have been amused by his posthumous popularity; as a young man he had complained: 'Isn't politics a dirty game? . . . all the promises to end tyranny, all the rattling of dead men's bones – in causes for which they never fought – all to no purpose.'[20]

Although Ryan's fame has grown in recent decades, he has also been the subject of increasingly hostile historiographical assessment, only recently being labelled a proponent of a 'Gaelic Vichy' and 'stool pigeon for the Nazis'.[21] A recent study equates the life of Frank Ryan with Eoin O'Duffy, 'men who hoped and worked for the victory of Hitler's New Order'.[22] Ryan's presence in Germany was deeply compromising, but such comments suggest an unwillingness to distinguish between utilising German support and sympathising with Nazism, an allegation for which there is no convincing evidence.

More convincing criticism has been made in Richard English's *Radicals and the Republic*, one of a number of studies to refute the assumption that socialism and republicanism are compatible. English argues that Ryan's presence in Germany demonstrated that the ideology of socialist republicans was fundamentally incoherent and disproves the claim that their movement was 'inherently progressive'.[23] Both of these points are valid, but should be placed in a broader context. How widely believed was it that socialist republicanism – or any ideology for that matter – was 'inherently progressive'? Does Ryan's presence in Germany suggest that socialist republicanism was not a progressive ideology or that there was little difference between left republicanism – with its insistence on the need to win popular support through a socially progressive agenda – and the physical-force tradition? It should also be noted that Ryan's collaborationist stance was not representative of other leading socialist republicans such as O'Donnell and Gilmore. In assessing the appeal and significance of left republican-ism, its practical activism – trade union organisation, anti-fascism, campaigns against slum landlords, and other attempts to draw attention to the social injustice of 1930s Ireland – should be given as much consideration as the incoherent theories underlying the movement. While English's conclusion that the socialist republican ideology of the 1930s failed is demonstrably true, too much can be made of this. Time has not been much kinder to other ideologies of this period – whether European totalitarianism or the intransigent nationalism of de Valera and Craigavon. Although the Workers' Republic has never seemed more remote, if the broad thrust of left republicanism was to shift the republican movement from mili-tarism into a process of politicisation based on a socially radical agenda, the project cannot be entirely dismissed as a failure in light of Sinn Féin's electoral success in Northern Ireland since the 1990s.

Like much of the academic historiography of republicanism in recent decades, English's interest in figures such as Ryan is partly motivated by his concern that contemporary republicans have used 'their political ancestors as ammunition in their own struggles'.[24] Ironically, Ryan's legacy has also been used to legitimise the peace process. An article written in 1998 by Deaglán de Bréadún, the Northern editor of the *Irish Times*, approvingly placed the INLA ceasefire of that year in 'the same left-wing republican tradition as Frank Ryan'.[25] But whether one is seeking to decommission dead patriots or appropriate their legacy for eirenic purposes, it seems doubtful that contemporary political lessons can be drawn from Ryan's deeply inconsistent life. Shortly after Ryan's death George Gilmore told Rosamond Jacob that 'Frank was a man of action not a writer'.[26] After a life in political activism and journalism, it is revealing that Gilmore could make such a comment. Yet it rings true. Ryan never consistently stood for any identifiable ideology – he is as easily claimed by rival factions of the IRA as by the Communist Party. One of the most charismatic revolutionaries in Irish history, Ryan had many fine qualities – idealism, bravery, honour and a hatred of social injustice. But he was also zealous, intolerant, militaristic, and failed to sustain a coherent political analysis – oscillating between an unsophisticated Fenianism and internationalist socialism throughout his life. His legacy will continue to be claimed by those seeking a symbol for their cause, but this study suggests that Ryan, whose short but remarkable life spanned four brutal wars, is perhaps a better emblem of his times – a period of extraordinary turmoil and instability which produced idealism and violence in equal measure – than of any particular cause.

Notes

Chapter 1: *Republican, 1902–32*

1   Rosamond Jacob diary (hereafter RJD), 31 Jan. 1935 (NLI, MS 32582).
2   Ibid., 24 Jan. 1928.
3   Aodh Ó Canainn, 'Oral history: Eilís Ryan in her own words', *Saothar*, 21 (1996), p. 131.
4   RJD, 26 Sept. 1927, 4 Apr. 1945.
5   Seán Cronin, *Frank Ryan: The Search for the Republic* (Dublin, 1980), p. 21.
6   RJD, 10 July 1927, 13 Feb. 1929.
7   Ibid., 6 May 1927.
8   Ibid., 31 July, 2 Mar. 1929.
9   Ibid., 24 Nov. 1929.
10 Ibid., notes on 1929.
11 Ibid., 2 Aug., 18 Feb. 1930.
12 Ibid., 5, 22 Mar. 1926, 1 May 1927.
13 Quoted in Cronin, *Ryan*, p. 25.
14 Elizabeth (Budge) Clissmann, interview with author, 31 May 2000.
15 RJD, 13 Feb. 1929.
16 Ibid., 21 June 1927.
17 Ibid., 10 Mar. 1926.
18 Ibid., 2 Oct. 1926.
19 *An Phoblacht*, 21 Apr. 1928.
20 Quoted in J. P. McHugh, 'Voices of the rearguard: a study of *An Phoblacht*' (MA thesis, University College Dublin, 1983), p. 111.
21 Seachránaidhe, *Easter Week and After* (Dublin, 1928), pp. 7, 8, 16.
22 *An Phoblacht*, 18 Aug. 1928.
23 RJD, 28 Sept. 1928, 17 Nov. 1926, 27 July 1929.
24 RJD, 1 Feb. 1927.
25 Ryan to Jacob, 11 Sept. 1927 (NLI, MS 31130/1).
26 Mark Mazower, *Dark Continent* (London, 1998), pp. 20–1.

27 *An Phoblacht*, 19 May 1928.

28 Cronin, *Ryan*, p. 108.

29 *An Phoblacht*, 2 July 1926.

30 Richard English, *Radicals and the Republic – Socialist Republicanism in the Irish Free State, 1925–1937* (Oxford, 1994).

31 *An Phoblacht*, 5 Jan. 1929.

32 Ibid., 2 Apr. 1932.

33 Ibid., 21 Apr. 1928.

34 RJD, 18 June 1928.

35 Seachránaidhe, *Emancipation* (Dublin, 1929), pp. 9, 13, 15.

36 RJD, 24 Oct. 1933.

37 Cronin, *Ryan*, p. 24.

38 Chief Supt David Neligan to Secretary, Department of Justice, 11 Nov. 1930 (NAI, DJ 8/684).

39 *An Phoblacht*, 3 Nov. 1928.

40 Ibid., 31 Mar. 1928.

41 RJD, 11 Nov. 1926.

42 Special Branch report, 10 Nov. 1929 (NAI, DJ 8/682). Con Neenan described Ryan as the 'best speaker in Ireland' (NLI, MS 17467).

43 Special Branch report, 11 Nov. 1939 (NAI, DJ 8/682).

44 RJD, 8 July 1932.

45 *An Phoblacht*, 16 Nov. 1929.

46 Ibid., 28 Sept. 1929.

47 RJD, 13 Nov. 1926.

48 Kathleen Lynn diary, 8 Dec. 1931 (Royal College of Physicians Archives). I am grateful to Margaret Ó hÓgartaigh for this reference.

49 See miscellaneous police reports, 1928–34 (NAI, DJ 8/682; 684).

50 *An Phoblacht*, 15 Nov. 1930.

51 Ibid., 1 Sept. 1928.

52 O'Duffy, memo. to Minister for Justice (NAI, DJ 8/684).

53 Ryan to Jacob, 10 Sept. 1928 (NLI, MS 31130/1).

54 RJD, 7 Nov. 1928.

55 Ibid., 13 Feb. 1929.

56 Garda Commissioner, confidential report, 31 May 1931 (UCDA, P80/856).

57 Garda Commissioner, memo., 6 Dec. 1926 (NAI, DT S5260).

58 Quoted in Conor Brady, *Guardians of the Peace* (Dublin, 2000 edn), p. 152.

59 *An Phoblacht*, 7 Dec. 1929.

60 Garda Commissioner, confidential report, 5 July 1929 (UCDA, P24/477).

61 Secretary, Department of Justice, to Secretary, Executive Council, 26 Mar. 1928 (ibid, P80/851).

62 *An Phoblacht*, 26 Oct. 1929.

63 Ibid., 11 Jan. 1930.

64 Ibid., 2 Nov. 1929.

65 Cronin, *Ryan*, p. 25.

66 *An Phoblacht*, 7 Dec. 1929.

67 Cosgrave to Byrne, 19 Sept. 1931 (Dublin Diocesan Archives, Office of the President of the Executive Council and Taoiseach, 1931).

68 *Dáil Éireann deb.*, xl, 293 (15 Oct. 1931).

69 RJD, 11 Aug. 1931.

70 *Republican File*, 16 Jan. 1932.

Chapter 2: *Socialist Republican, 1932–6*

1 *An Phoblacht*, 19 Mar. 1932.

2 Rosamond Jacob diary (hereafter RJD), 13 Mar. 1932; *An Phoblacht*, 19 Mar. 1932; Department of Justice memo., 12 Mar. 1932 (NAI DJ 8/698).

3 *An Phoblacht*, 12 Mar. 1932,

4 Aodh Ó Canainn, 'Oral history: Eilís Ryan in her own words', *Saothar*, 21 (1996), p. 134; RJD, 14 Mar. 1932.

5 *An Phoblacht*, 4 June 1932.

6 Gilmore to Chairman of Army Council, 16 Sept. 1932 (UCDA P69/53/368).

7 *An Phoblacht*, 27 Aug. 1932.

8 Quoted in Richard English, *Radicals and the Republic – Socialist Republicanism in the Irish Free State, 1925–1937* (Oxford, 1994), p. 136.

9 RJD, 25 May 1932.

10 Special Branch report, 11 Nov. 1932 (NAI, DJ 8/684).

11 RJD, 12 Nov. 1932.

12 Unsigned Department of Justice memo. to President, *c*.Nov. 1932 (NAI, DJ 8/684).

13 *An Phoblacht*, 19 Nov. 1932; RJD, 28 Apr. 1936.

14 Memo. to Army Council, 5 Nov. 1932 (UCDA P69/53/183); Chairman of Army Council to Editor, *An Phoblacht*, 29 Oct. 1932 (ibid., P69/53/188); Chairman to Army Council, 20 Oct. 1932 (ibid., P69/53/190).

15 Seán Cronin, *Frank Ryan: The Search for the Republic* (Dublin, 1980), p. 46.

16 Ryan to Twomey, 5 Feb. 1933 (UCDA, P69/53/179).

17 Twomey to Ryan, 3 Mar. 1933 (ibid., P69/53/177).

18 MacBride to Ryan, 3 Mar. 1933 (ibid., P69/53/178).

19 Gilmore to Army Council, Sept. 1932 (ibid., P69/53/368).

20 Adjutant-General to Twomey, 23 Mar. 1933 (ibid., P69/53/152).

21 Minutes of General Army Conference, 1933 (ibid., P69/187).

22 Ryan to Twomey, 23 Mar. 1933 (ibid., P69/53/175).

23 Twomey to Sheehy Skeffington, 31 Mar. 1933 (ibid., P69/53/170).

24 Sheehy Skeffington to Twomey, 2 Apr. 1933 (ibid., P69/53/167).

25 RJD, 3 Apr. 1933.

26 Ibid., 19 June 1932.

27 Ibid., 8 Apr. 1933.

28 Ibid., 20 May 1933.

29 RJD, 31 May 1933; miscellaneous correspondence between Staff Captain O'Reilly (Ryan) and Adjutant General and Chief of Staff, 9 Jan. 1933 (UCDA, P106/2038/1–11).

30 For Gilmore see RJD, 25 Feb. 1932, 8 Apr. 1933, 9 Jan. 1934.

31 O/C Dublin Brigade to Chief of Staff, 9 Jan. 1933 (UCDA, P69/53/252); Intelligence Officer, Dublin Brigade, to Director of Intelligence, 21 Dec. 1932 (ibid., P69/53/254). Ryan reportedly claimed O'Donnell was a communist (Adjutant General to Chief of Staff, 23 Mar. 1933 (ibid. P69/53/152)).

32 Minutes of General Army Convention, 1934 (ibid., P67/525).

33 *Republican Congress*, 9 Nov. 1935.

34 Ibid., 9 June 1934.

35 Ibid., 18 Aug. 1934.

36 Constitution of the Irish Citizen Army, 1934 (NAI, DJ 8/320).

37 Patrick Byrne, *The Irish Republican Congress Revisited* (London, 1994), p. 16.

38 Another example of this was *Republican Congress*'s (11 Jan. 1936) headline trumpeting the formation of four 'Active Service Units'. The small print, however, revealed these would be involved in such activities as the organisation of 'outings, collections and classes'.

39 *An Phoblacht*, 5 May 1934; *Republican Congress*, 19 May 1934.

40 *Republican Congress*, 26 May 1934.

41 Ibid.

42 J. Bowyer Bell, *The Secret Army* (Dublin, 1997 edn), p. 114.

43 *An Phoblacht*, 21 Apr. 1934.

44 Peter O'Connor, *A Soldier of Liberty* (Dublin, 1996), pp. 9–10.

45 Joseph O'Connor, *Even the Olives are Bleeding* (Dublin, 1992), p. 50.

46 *Republican Congress*, 16 June 1934.

47 *An Phoblacht*, 23 June 1934.

48 *Republican Congress*, 23 June 1934.

49 Sheila Humphreys and Eithne Coyle to Republican Congress Committee, 18 July 1934 (UCDA, P106/1490).

50 *Republican Congress*, 23 June 1934; cited in J. P. McHugh, 'Voices of the rearguard: a study of *An Phoblacht*' (MA thesis, University College Dublin, 1983), pp. 127–8.

51 *Republican Congress*, 1 Sept. 1934.

52 Cronin, *Ryan*, p. 58.

53 Quoted ibid., p. 65.

54 Department of Justice, 'Notes on Republican Congress', *c.*1936, p. 13 (UCDA, P67/527).

55 Miscellaneous correspondence between Kilkenny branch of ICA and rival ICA GHQs, Nov.–Dec. 1934 (NAI, DJ 8/320).

56 Quoted in Cronin, *Ryan*, p. 72.

57 English, *Radicals and the Republic*, p. 240.

58 RJD, 23 June 1935.

59 Special Branch report, 2 May 1935 (NAI DJ 8/386).

60 Cronin, *Ryan*, p. 66.

61 RJD, 14 Apr. 1936.

62 Ibid.; Cronin, *Ryan*, p. 66.

63 RJD, 18 Apr. 1936.

64 Quoted in Cronin, *Ryan*, p. 65.

Chapter 3: *Anti-fascist, 1936–8*

1 Quoted in Seán Cronin, *Frank Ryan: The Search for the Republic* (Dublin, 1980), p. 78.

2 *Irish Press*, 21 Sept. 1936.

3 Ibid., 22 Sept. 1936.

4 *Irish Independent*, 14 Dec. 1936.

5 Ryan to Kerney, Dec. 1939 (NAI, D/FA A20/3).

6 Quoted in James Hopkins, *Into the Heart of the Fire: the British in Spanish Civil War* (Stanford, 1998), pp. 368, 139.

7 Rosamond Jacob diary (hereafter RJD), 8 Oct. 1936.

8 Aodh Ó Canainn, 'Oral history: Eilís Ryan in her own words', *Saothar*, 21 (1996), p. 135.

9 Joe Monks, *With the Reds in Andalusia* (London, n.d.), p. 2.

10 Ibid., pp. 7–8.

11 Cronin, *Ryan*, p. 84.

12 Ryan, circular, 1 Jan. 1937 (Spanish Civil War file, Irish Labour History Society archives, Beggars' Bush Barracks, Dublin).

13 Cronin, *Ryan*, p. 91.

14 Robert A. Stradling, *The Irish and the Spanish Civil War 1936–1939* (Manchester, 1999), pp. 157–8.

15 Quoted in Cronin, *Ryan*, p. 67; Hopkins, *Into the Heart*, p. 169.

16 Peter Kerrigan, taped interview, 1976 (Imperial War Museum, Sound Archives, Spanish Civil War Collection, 810/6).

17 Hopkins, *Into the Heart*, p. 217.

18 Paul Preston, *Franco: A Biography* (London, 1995 edn), p. 222.

19 Stradling, *The Irish and the Spanish Civil War*, p. 163.

20 Hugh Thomas, *The Spanish Civil War* (London, 1990 edn), p. 591.

21 Monks, *With the Reds*, p. 22.

22 Quoted in Cronin, *Ryan*, p. 96.

23 Quoted ibid., p. 98.

24 Hopkins, *Into the Heart*, p. 245.

25 RJD, 30 Apr. 1937.

26 Quoted in Cronin, *Ryan*, p. 113.

27 Quoted in Hopkins, *Into the Heart*, p. 174.

28 Quoted in Cronin, *Ryan*, p. 130.

29 Ryan to Desmond Ryan, 11 June 1937 (UCDA, LA10 Q/19/2).

30 Cronin, *Ryan*, p. 114.

31 Ryan to Kerney, *c.*Dec. 1940 (NAI, D/FA A20/3).

32 Nora Harkin, interview with author, June 1996.

33 Quoted in Cronin, *Ryan*, p. 115.

34 Stradling, *The Irish and the Spanish Civil War*, p. 154.

35 Eugene Downing, interview with author, Jan. 1996.

36 Cronin, *Ryan*, p. 114.

37 Fearghal McGarry, *Irish Politics and the Spanish Civil War* (Cork, 1999), p. 69.

38 Ibid., p. 79. See Hopkins, *Into the Heart* (pp. 266–90), for the treatment of 'political unreliables' in the British battalion. At least one Irish volunteer in the International Brigades, Maurice Ryan, was executed. Although accused of fascist sympathies and espionage, and previously jailed for 'disruption', the erratic battlefield behaviour which ultimately sealed his fate was more likely a result of drunkenness. Hopkins mistakenly claimed that William Meeke, a labourer from County Antrim, was shot for desertion. Although imprisoned in Spain, Meeke was subsequently repatriated. Richard Baxell, whose research suggests that the level of Comintern control within the British battalion (and the resulting disaffection) has been overstated by Hopkins, estimates that at least two volunteers in the battalion were executed, while a further two were placed 'in positions that virtually guaranteed their deaths' (*British Volunteers in the Spanish Civil War: The British Battalion in the International Brigades,*

1936–1939 (London, 2004), pp. 134–40). For the fate of another Irish victim of Stalinism in Republican Spain (Brian Goold-Verschoyle), see Barry McLoughlin's *Left to the Wolves: Irish Victims of Stalinist Terror*(Dublin, 2007).

39 Photocopy of file contents, RGASPI (Comintern Archive, Moscow, 545/6/445), provided by Barry McLoughlin.

40 Eugene Downing, interview with author, Jan. 1996.

41 Ryan to Alonzo Elliot, 28 Mar. 38 (RGASPI, 545/6/129). My thanks to Barry McLoughlin for sharing his Moscow research.

42 Cronin, *Ryan*, pp. 123–4, 129.

43 Ryan to Kerney, *c.*Dec. 1939, enclosed in Kerney to Walsh, 9 Jan. 1940 (NAI, DFA A20/3).

44 Unsigned document, *c.*1938 (NLI, MS 33132).

Chapter 4: *Collaborator, 1938–44*

1 Ryan to Kerney, *c.*Jan. 1940 (NAI, DFA A20/3).

2 Kerney to Walshe, 7 May 1940 (ibid.).

3 Statement by C. Kent, 15 Nov. 1938, enclosed in Charlotte Haldane to de Valera, 16 Nov. 1938 (NAI, DFA A20).

4 Kerney to Walshe, 3 Oct. 1938 (ibid.).

5 Ibid., 2 June 1938 (NAI, DFA 244/22).

6 Ryan to Kerney, *c.*Dec. 1939, enclosed in Kerney to Walshe, 9 Jan. 1940 (ibid., DFA A20/3).

7 Kerney to Walshe, 17 June 1939 (ibid., DFA A20/2).

8 Ibid., *c.*14 Sept. 1939 (ibid.).

9 Ryan to Kerney, *c.*Dec. 1939, enclosed in Kerney to Walshe, 9 Jan. 1940 (NAI, DFA A20/3).

10 Kerney to Walshe, 17 June 1939 (ibid.).

11 Ibid., 11 Aug. 1938 (NAI, DFA A20).

12 Ibid., 23 Dec. 1939 (ibid., DFA A20/3).

13 Ibid., 10 Oct. 1938 (ibid, DFA A20).

14 Ibid., 27 Nov. 1939 (ibid., DFA A20/3).

15 Kerney to Boland, 17 June 1939 (ibid, DFA A20/2).

16 Kerney to Walshe, 22 Aug. 1938 (ibid., DFA A20).

17 Ibid., 8 Oct. 1938 (ibid.).

18 Ibid., 6 July 1939 (NAI, DFA A20/2).

19 Ibid., 21 Nov. 1939 (ibid., DFA A20/3).

20 Col. Dan Bryan, G2, to Walshe, 6 Dec. 1940 (ibid., DFA A20/4); Kerney to Walshe, 27 Dec. 1939 (ibid., DFA A20/3).

21 Kerney to Walshe, 28 Dec. 1938 (ibid., DFA A20).

22 Ibid., 23 Apr. 1940 (ibid., DFA A20/3).

23 Ibid., 5 Oct. 1939 (ibid.).

24 Ibid., 5 Dec. 1939; 2 Feb. 1940 (ibid.).

25 Ibid., 17 June 1939 (NAI, DFA A20/2).

26 Ibid., 3, 8 Apr. 1940 (ibid., DFA A20/3).

27 Ibid., 27 Dec. 1939 (ibid.).

28 Ibid., 17 June 1939 (NAI, DFA A20/2).

29 Ibid., 2 Dec. 1938 (ibid., DFA A20).

30 Tom Jones, 'Recollections of Frank Ryan', pp. 4, 7, 8 (Marx Memorial Library, London, International Brigade Association Archives, box 28, G/13).

31 Kerney to Walshe, 26 Jan. 1940 (NAI, DFA A20/3).

32 Ibid., 26 Aug. 1940 (ibid., DFA A20/4).

33 Cronin, relying largely on the evidence of Helmut Clissmann, believed that de Valera approved Ryan's release (Seán Cronin, *Frank Ryan: The Search for the Republic* (Dublin, 1980), p. 162), as does Tim Pat Coogan, *De Valera: Long Fellow, Long Shadow* (London, 1993), p. 617. Coogan was told by F. H. Boland, an authoritative source given his role as Secretary of the Department of External Affairs from 1946–50, that de Valera sanctioned Ryan's release through non-official channels (Tim Pat Coogan, interview with author, 13 Feb. 2001). Dermot Keogh (*Ireland and Europe, 1919–1948* (Dublin 1988), p. 155) considers it unlikely, while Eunan O'Halpin (*Defending Ireland: The Irish State and its Enemies since 1922* (Oxford, 1999), p. 194) attributed Ryan's release to Kerney's 'hopeless judgement'. For a sympathetic account of Kerney's actions, see www.leopoldhkerney.com.

34 Department of Defence, memo. on Frank Ryan, 20 Oct. 1941 (Irish Military Archives, Cathal Brugha Barracks, Dublin (G2/0257, Part I)).

35 Elizabeth Clissmann, interview with author, 31 May 2000.

36 Ibid.

37 Department of Defence, memo. on Frank Ryan, 20 Oct. 1941 (Irish Military Archives, G2/0257).

38 Gerald O'Reilly to Helen O'Reilly, 26 Mar. 1940 (NAI, DFA A20/4).

39 Operations order for U-37, 22 Jan. 1940; Abwehr II Kriegstagebuch, 3, 6, 8, 26 Aug. 1940 (both in possession of Mark Hull). I am grateful to Mark Hull for generously sharing his research in the German archives.

40 Part 1, Appendix A, Kurt Haller file, p. xvii (PRO, KV 2/769). My thanks to Eunan O'Halpin for this reference.

41 Department of External Affairs, memo. of interview with Elizabeth Clissmann, 6 June 1946 (NAI, DFA A20 annexe).

42 Elizabeth Clissmann, interview with author, 31 May 2000.

43 Quoted in Cronin, *Ryan*, p. 43.

44 Ryan to Kerney, 11 Dec. 1940 (NAI, DFA A20/4). The tone of this letter, and that of other correspondence between both men, suggests that Ryan believed that Kerney had acted independently to secure his release without the authority of his own government.

45 Ryan to Kerney, 6 Nov. 1941 (ibid.).

46 Ibid.

47 Ibid., 11 Dec. 1940 (NAI, DFA A20/4).

48 Ibid., 6. Nov. 1941 (ibid.).

49 *Documents on German Foreign Policy*, Series D, Vol. XIII, pp. 364–6 (24 Aug. 1941). I am grateful to Mark Hull for this reference.

50 Lahousen diary, 21 Aug. 1941 (PRO, KV 2/173).

51 Ryan to Kerney, 13 Aug. 1942 (NAI, DFA A20/4).

52 Ibid., 14 Jan. 1942 (ibid.).

53 Ibid.

54 F. H. Boland, memo., 8 July 1944 (NAI, DFA A20 annexe)

55 Ryan to Kerney, 14 May 1942 (ibid., DFA A20/4).

56 Ibid., 13 Aug. 1942 (ibid.).

57 Ibid., 14 May 1942 (ibid).

58 Quoted in David O'Donoghue, *Hitler's Irish Voices: The Story of German Radio's Wartime Irish Service* (Belfast, 1998), p. 58.

59 Ibid., pp. 51–2.

60 Brendan Barrington (ed.), *The Wartime Broadcasts of Francis Stuart 1942–44* (Dublin, 2000).

61 John Codd, memo., 'Frank Richards *alias* Mr Moloney', July 1945 (Military Archives, G2/0257, Appendix 2).

62 Enno Stephan, *Spies in Ireland* (London, 1965 edn), pp. 216–17.

63 O'Donoghue, *Hitler's Irish Voices*, p. 99.

64 Ibid., p. 145.

65 Francis Stuart, interview with David O'Donoghue, 24 Feb. 1990.

66 Quoted in O'Donoghue, *Hitler's Irish Voices*, pp. 152–3.

67 Kerney to F. H. Boland, 6 July 1944 (NAI, DFA A20/4).

68 F. H. Boland, memo., 8 July 1944 (ibid., DFA A20 annexe). De Valera's understandable concern to safeguard Irish neutrality by denying both the Allied and Axis powers any pretext for aggression against Éire points to the implausibility of the claim that Ryan was present in Germany as de Valera's 'de facto and effective Ambassador in Berlin' (Manus O'Riordan, 'Frank Ryan – Collaborator?', *Irish Literary Supplement*, Fall 2003). On the contrary, Ryan's

presence in Berlin, a cause of considerable concern to MI5, jeopardised Irish neutrality by furnishing Britain's intelligence agencies with evidence of IRA collaboration that could have been used to justify a British invasion of Éire during the period of the German invasion threat. See Eunan O'Halpin, *Spying on Ireland: British Intelligence and Irish Neutrality During the Second World War* (Oxford, 2008), p. 124.

69 Francis Stuart, interview with David O'Donoghue, 17 Nov. 1989. I am grateful to David O'Donoghue for granting access to his interviews.

70 Telegram, Iverna to Estero, 18 Feb. 1945 (NAI, DFA A20/4). Stroke can be a symptom of syphilis, but Ryan and his brothers had a history of blood pressure and heart problems.

71 Memo. by Professor De Crinis, Direktor der Klinik, Charité Hospital, Berlin, 2 Feb. 1945 (ibid.).

72 J. P. Duggan, *Herr Hempel at the German Legation in Dublin 1937–45* (DLitt. thesis, Trinity College Dublin, 1979), p. 421.

Conclusion

1 Ryan has been the subject of three biographies and several documentaries including 'Let my Tombstone be of Granite' (RTÉ, 1979) and 'Seamróg agus Swastica' (Akajava, 2002). He has inspired several characters in novels and movies, including that of Liam Devlin in Jack Higgins's thriller *The Eagle Has Landed* (1975). He features in such songs as Christy Moore's 'Viva La Quinta Brigada' (*Ride On*, WEA, 1984) and 'The Sickbed of Cúchulainn' by The Pogues (*Rum, Sodomy & the Lash*, Stiff Records, 1985). His continued appeal is also evidenced by the availability of Frank Ryan T-shirts and other memorabilia on radical websites, and the existence of the Frank Ryan Society in University College Dublin.

2 Robert A. Stradling, *The Irish and the Spanish Civil War 1936–1939* (Manchester, 1999), p. 2.

3 Eunan O'Halpin, *Defending Ireland* (Oxford, 1999), p. 196.

4 *Reynolds News*, 6 Aug. 1944.

5 *Irish Freedom*, Dec. 1944; *Canadian Tribune*, quoted in *Irish Democrat*, Aug. 1945.

6 O'Donnell and Sheehy Skeffington in *Irish Times*, 9 Mar. 1945.

7 Rosamond Jacob diary (hereafter RJD), 8 Oct. 1945, notes on 1945. Drafts of the short biography, written by Rosamund Jacob, are held in the National Library (Jacob Papers, MS 33132) and the UCD Archives (O'Donoghue-Humphreys Papers, P106/1711).

8   Seán Cronin, *Frank Ryan: The Search for the Republic* (Dublin, 1980), pp. 205, 191.

9   Margaret Ward, *Hanna Sheehy Skeffington: A Life* (Cork, 1997), p. 322; Peter Hegarty, *Peadar O'Donnell* (Dublin, 1999), p. 239. Another recent account attributed Ryan's decision to return to Germany to 'a [nervous] breakdown accompanied by a belief that he [Ryan] would only feel safe again in the care of [Helmut] Clissmann' (Manus O'Riordan, 'Frank Ryan – Collaborator?', *Irish Literary Supplement*, Fall 2003).

10   Michael McInerney, 'The enigma of Frank Ryan', *The Old Limerick Journal*, I: 2 (1979), p. 34; Michael O'Riordan, *Connolly Column* (Dublin, 1979), pp. 151–8; O'Riordan, interview with Eileen Battersby, *Irish Times*, 15 Apr. 1999: 'He was a great man; he never collaborated with the Nazis, we know this.' J. Bowyer Bell, *The Secret Army: The IRA 1916–1979* (Dublin, 1979 edn), p. 197, referred to 'Ryan's continuing anti-Nazi stand during his German exile', while Conor Foley, *Legion of the Rearguard: the IRA and the Modern Irish State* (London, 1992), p. 198, argued that Ryan's co-operation with Germany fell into 'a unique category' which did not constitute collaboration. The first edition of this biography was criticised by Sinn Féin's general secretary, Robbie Smyth, as 'deeply flawed' on the basis that it described Ryan as a collaborator without 'firm evidence', adding: 'The truth of the matter is that Ryan acted as an intermediary between the IRA and Nazi Germany while he was held captive by the latter' (*An Phoblacht*, 27 June 2003). In fact, the sources cited in that book to support the claim that Ryan returned voluntarily to Germany with the intention, under specific circumstances, of facilitating some form of collaboration between Irish republicans and Nazi Germany, included the records of German military intelligence, the records of the German Foreign Office, Irish military intelligence (G2) reports, the testimony of the Irish Minister in Spain, Leopold Kerney, the reports of the Irish Department of External Affairs, MI5 reports, the testimony of all the major figures involved with Ryan (including Veesenmayer, Kerney, and the Clissmanns) as well as Ryan's personal correspondence from Germany to Leopold Kerney. It was also confirmed by the testimony of the sole remaining living witness, Elizabeth Clissmann.

11   Although commemorations continue to be held by both (Provisional) Sinn Féin and Republican Sinn Féin at the site of Russell's statue in Fairview Park, Dublin, it has become one of the most frequently vandalised memorials in the Irish Republic. Following its decapitation by self-proclaimed anti-fascists in 2004, the original statue was replaced in 2009 by a solid bronze statue fitted with motion sensors and a GPS tracking device located in Russell's head, precautions which have failed to deter further attacks.

12 Cronin, *Ryan*, p. 11.

13 *Irish Workers' Weekly*, 28 Sept. 1940.

14 Irish Workers' League to Zentralkomitee, Sozialistische Einheitspartei, DDR, 12 Mar. 1961 (Marx Memorial Library, International Brigade Association Archives, Box 28, File G).

15 Department of External Affairs, memo. on repatriation of Ryan's remains, 1966 (NAI, DFA A20).

16 Aodh Ó Canainn, 'Oral history: Eilís Ryan in her own words', *Saothar*, 21 (1996), p. 142.

17 *Irish Times*, 20 June 1979.

18 Ibid., 23 June 1979.

19 Ibid., 21, 25 June 1979.

20 Ryan to Jacob, 11 Sept. 1927 (NLI, MS 31130/1).

21 Quoted in Enda Staunton, 'Frank Ryan & collaboration: a reassessment', *History Ireland*, v, no. 3 (1997), p. 50.

22 Stradling, *The Irish and the Spanish Civil War*, p. 3.

23 Richard English, 'Socialist Republicanism in independent Ireland, 1922–49', in Mike Cronin and John Regan (eds), *Ireland: The Politics of Independence, 1922–49* (Basingstoke, 2000), p. 93; Richard English, *Radicals and the Republic – Socialist Republicanism in the Irish Free State, 1925–1937* (Oxford, 1994), pp. 245–51.

24 Richard English, 'Radicals and the Republic: Socialist Republicanism in the Irish Free State 1925–37' (PhD thesis, University of Keele, 1990), p. 5.

25 Deaglán de Bréadún, 'Pipes audible only to the faithful?', *Irish Times*, 24 Aug. 1998.

26 RJD, 14 Mar. 1945.

Select Bibliography

PRIMARY SOURCES

For Ryan's family background see Aodh Ó Canainn, 'Oral history: Eilís Ryan in her own words', *Saothar*, 21 (1996), pp. 129–46. The records of the departments of Justice, the Taoiseach and External Affairs in the National Archives cited throughout this study provide a wealth of detail on Ryan. Rosamond Jacob's papers in the National Library are a valuable source for Ryan and the radical republican milieu of inter-war Dublin. For IRA activism see the collection of interviews in Uinseann MacEoin's *The IRA in the Twilight Years, 1923–1948* (Dublin, 1997). Ryan's political writings can be found in numerous inter-war radical newspapers, particularly those under his editorship including *An Phoblacht*, *Republican Congress*, *Irish People* and the *Irish Democrat*. Sources for Ryan in Spain include the Imperial War Museum's Spanish Civil War oral history collection and the records of the International Brigade Association in the Marx Memorial Library (both in London). Ryan's imprisonment in Spain and activities in Nazi Germany are detailed in the National Archives' D/FA A20 collection, the Irish Military Archives' G2 collection and MI5's KV series in the Public Record Office, London.

SECONDARY SOURCES

Seán Cronin's *Frank Ryan: The Search for the Republic* (Dublin, 1980) is a well detailed if essentially uncritical biography. More critical reflections on the ideological inconsistencies which beset inter-war left republicanism are provided by Richard English's *Radicals and the Republic: Socialist Republicans in the Irish Free State, 1925–1937* (Oxford, 1994). Tim Pat Coogan's *The IRA* (London, 1970) surveys the history of the Irish Republican Army from its origins to the recent Troubles, while Brian Murphy's *Patrick Pearse and the Lost Republican Ideal* (Dublin, 1990) provides an insightful, if partisan, analysis of the legitimist republican tradition. Tom Garvin's *Nationalist Revolutionaries in Ireland, 1858–1928* (Oxford, 1987) reconstructs a republican mentality of which Ryan can be seen as an archetypal example. Donal Ó Drisceoil's biography, *Peadar O'Donnell* (Cork, 2001), offers a sympathetic assessment of Ryan's political mentor. Irish involvement in Spain is detailed in Michael O'Riordan's *Connolly Column* (Dublin 1979), Bill Alexander's *British Volunteers for Liberty* (London, 1982) and, more critically, James Hopkins's thoughtful *Into the Heart of the Fire: The British in the Spanish Civil War* (Stanford, 1998), Robert A. Stradling's *The Irish and the Spanish Civil War, 1936–1939* (Manchester, 1999) and Fearghal McGarry's *Irish Politics and the Spanish Civil War* (Cork, 1999). For the broader diplomatic and security picture see Dermot Keogh's *Ireland and Europe, 1919–1948* (Dublin, 1988) and Eunan O'Halpin's *Defending Ireland: The Irish State and its Enemies since 1922* (Oxford, 1999). Interesting recent accounts of the Irish in Germany include David O'Donoghue's *Hitler's Irish Voices: The Story of German Radio's Wartime Irish Service* (Belfast, 1998) and *The Wartime Broadcasts of Francis Stuart, 1942–1944*, edited by Brendan Barrington (Dublin, 2000).

RECENT PUBLICATIONS

Since this book was first published in 2002, a great deal of new material on radicalism in inter-war Ireland has appeared, as has another (sympathetic) biography of Frank Ryan: Adrian Hoar's *In Green and Red: The Lives of Frank Ryan* (Dingle, 2004). Brian Hanley's excellent study, *The IRA, 1926–36* (Dublin, 2002), sheds much new light on the inter-war IRA. Previous surveys of the IRA by Tim Pat Coogan and others have been superseded by Richard English's *Armed Struggle: A History of the IRA* (London, 2003). Fearghal McGarry's *Eoin O'Duffy: A Self-Made Hero* (Oxford, 2007) assesses the life of Frank Ryan's political nemesis. Irish links with international communism are explored in Emmet O'Connor's *Reds and the Green: Ireland, Russia and the Communist Internationals, 1919–43* (Dublin, 2004) and Barry McLoughlin's *Left to the Wolves: Irish Victims of Stalinist Terror* (Dublin, 2007). Much new information on the British battalion, the unit in which Frank Ryan and most other Irish volunteers in Spain fought in, is contained in Richard Baxell's *British Volunteers in the Spanish Civil War: The British Battalion in the International Brigades, 1936–1939* (London, 2004). The IRA's murky contacts with Nazi

Germany have been comprehensively detailed in Mark Hull's *German Espionage in Ireland, 1939–1945* (Dublin, 2003). The efforts of British intelligence agencies to cope with the wartime threat posed by both the IRA and the neutral Irish State are authoritatively assessed in *Spying on Ireland: British Intelligence and Irish Neutrality during the Second World War* by Eunan O'Halpin (Oxford, 2008).

Index